HISTORY

OF

GRAND RAPIDS,

WITH

BIOGRAPHICAL SKETCHES.

BY

CHAS. RICHARD TUTTLE

AUTHOR "ILLUSTRATED HISTORY OF MICHIGAN."

GRAND RAPIDS:
PUBLISHED BY TUTTLE & COONEY.
HORTON BROS. & CO., GENERAL AGENTS.
Printed at the Democrat Office, Grand Rapids, Mich.
1874.

S.B.N.-0-912382-15-5   L.O.C.-73-93481

Reprinted 1974

By

BLACK LETTER PRESS
Grand Rapids, Michigan

Cover Art: Robert Nelson

PREFACE.

My labors in connection with the "History of Michigan" have forcibly suggested the propriety of editing a series of small volumes, embracing, separately, the histories of the principal cities of the Northwest. There is very much valuable and interesting narrative connected with the early settlement of this country which cannot well be embraced in a general history of the State or States, and yet this history, or these local traditions should be preserved.

It will no doubt be a pleasing entertainment for the readers of Grand Rapids and Kent county to go back to the early days of Michigan civilization, when the first footprints of the white man were made on the valley of the Grand River, and then to follow the interesting events in the history of the place, in a pleasant style of narrative, down to the present time. The treaties between the Americans and the savages, the midnight massacres, the bloody deeds of Indian treachery, the romance of pioneer life, the thrilling tales of adventure and escape, the legends of the savages and lastly, the great resources and rapid development of

the city,—all these combine to render the narrative
pleasing to the reader and valuable to the family library.

In conclusion, the publishers desire to tender their
thanks to the proprietors of the Grand Rapids *Democrat*
and especially to the men employed in the book department of their printing house, for the pains-taking care
and mechanical skill displayed in carrying this work
through to completion; and also to the press of Grand
Rapids for their favorable comments.

CHARLES R. TUTTLE.

Detroit, Jan. 1874,

HISTORY OF GRAND RAPIDS.

CHAPTER I.

Indian Villages of the Owastenong—Their Appearance and Condition in 1760—A grand War Council-Speech of Pontiac—Departure of the Warriors for the Seige of Detroit.

Owashtenong, or the rapids of the Grand River, was, for many years, the center of savage intercourse in northwestern Michigan. A densly populated village of the Ottawas was located on the west side of the river, about a quarter of a mile below the rapids, and is spoken of in various works on the Indian tribes of the Northwest, as having reached its greatest strength and influence about the year 1760. At this period the settlement is said to have been the home of some three thousands souls, although it is not probable that so large a number resided there permanently.

At a later period there were several Indian villages in the vicinity of the rapids—one of the Chippewas, one of the Pottawattamies, and another of a mixed population of various tribes. The Chippewas who came to settle here were of that portion of this nation who became, at this period, a part of the great Indian confederation organized under the influence of Pontiac, the Ottawa chief.

It is not our purpose here to enter into a complete detail of the important events in the history of these Indian villages, but the reader will, no doubt, be entertained with a brief notice of their condition and customs at that period at which our narrative commences.

The life of the Indians in this vicinity, though utterly void of those many phases which vary the routine of civilized existence, was one of considerable excitement. The chase, the war path, the dance, the festival, the game of hazard, the race of political ambition, all had their votaries. When the assembled sachems had resolved on assisting the great Pontiac in the seige of Detroit, in 1761, and when, from their great councilhouse of bark in the Valley of the Owashtenong, their

---

deputies had gone forth to invite other warriors to arms, then all along the banks of the Grand River, a thousand war-like hearts caught up the summons with savage enthusiasm.

With feasting and praying, and consulting dreams and omens; with invoking the war-god, and dancing the frantic war dance, the warriors sought to insure the triumph of their arms in the contest to which they had been summoned.

We will stop here to look in upon the great war council held in the valley of the Grand River, at the village of the Ottawas, in the spring of 1761, at which Pontiac himself was present. The great Ottawa chief came with his squaws and children, and was received by the sachems with tokens of their greatest reverence for this powerful warrior. Band after band came straggling in from every side, until the valley for nearly a mile was dotted with their slender wigwams. Here were idle warriors, smoking and laughing in groups, or beguiling the lazy hours with gambling, with feasting, or with doubtful stories of their own exploits. Here and there could be seen youthful gallants, brilliant with all the foppery of beads, feathers and hawks' bills, but held, as yet, in light esteem, since they had slain no enemy, and taken no scalp; young damsels, radiant with bear's oil and vermilion, and accomplished in all the arts of forest coquetry. The scene was also enlivened by troops of children, with small, black, mischevous eyes, roaming along the outskirts of the woods.

The council took place early in April. On that morning, several old men, known as the heralds of the camp, passed to and fro among the lodges calling the warriors, in a loud voice. In accordance with this summons they came forth from their cabins—the Ottawas, wrapped in their gaudy blankets; the Chippewas, fluttering in painted shirts, with their heads adorned with feathers. All were soon seated in a wide circle upon the grass, row inside of row, a sober, silent assembly. "Each savage countenance," says the historian, "seemed carved in wood, and none could have detected the deep and fiery passions hidden beneath that immovable exterior. Pipes, with ornamented stems, were lighted, and passed from hand to hand."

Then Pontiac rose and walked to the center of the ring. After taking a careful survey of his savage auditors, he began to speak. He opened his address by setting forth the arrogance, rapacity and injustice of the English, and contrasted their deeds with those of the French. He declared that the British commandant at Detroit had treated him with neglect and contempt; that the soldiers of that garrison had abused the Indians, and if left alone, would soon come to drive his peaceful hearers from their homes around this beautiful *Owashtenong*.

He fully set forth the danger that would arise to his people should the English gain supremacy. They had expelled the French, and would soon turn upon the Indians. He then displayed a broad belt of wampum, stating that he had received it from their great father, the King of France, who would soon come to their assistance.

After rousing in his listeners their native thirst for blood and vengeance, he next addressed himself to their superstitions. Here he related a curious tale, which had formed the conclusion of many former speeches delivered by this wonderful Indian for the purpose of gaining the friendship and support of savage warriors.

Many other speeches were, doubtless, made in the same council but no record of them has been preserved. All present were eager to march to Detroit and attack the garrison. The assembly now dissolved, and all the evening the women were busily engaged loading the canoes, which were drawn up on the back of the river just below the rapids. At an early hour the following morning the encampment broke 'up, and when the sun arose, more than fifty canoes, filled with warriors, could be seen floating slowly down the river toward the lake. They were following their gallant Ottawa leader to the seige of Detroit.

CHAPTER II.

Annual Gatherings in the Valley of the Grand River—A Great Feast in the Spring of 1674—Preparations for the Feast—Cooking—The Purification—The Assembly.

EVERY spring, after the hunt was over, a large number of Indians of the Ottawa, Pottawatamie, Chippewa, and other tribes, were accustomed to return to the vicinity of the rapids of the Grand River, and here, in the spring of 1764, one of their most memorable annual feasts was celebrated. Again the valley of the Grand Rapids was thickly dotted with curious wigwams, and in every quarter for more than half a mile a busy scene was presented. On this particular occasion, it is stated that more than four thousand Indians—men women and children—assembled to have their annual *pow-wow*. No sooner had the multitude collected than they began preparations. A curiously shaped, oblong tent was erected near the site of what was afterwards known as the Baptist Mission. It was about thirty feet long and twenty wide. A large quantity of bark was collected and placed in huge piles near at hand, to be used as a covering for the tent in the event of rain. This work performed, they next made three small excavations near each other in the middle of the tent, and after filling them with hard, round stones, fires were built upon them and kept burning constantly for three days. In the meantime small tents were being put up in rows, extending up and down the west bank of the river for a considerable distance. These rows of wigwams were about thirty feet apart, thus affording a splendid thoroughfare between them. All along on either side of this broad avenue, fires were built and kettles placed over them containing a variety of savage delicacies, such as sturgeon, sturgeon eggs, venison, and such game as the country afforded. In a majority of instances the cooking was conducted after the rudest manner, and the dishes served up were of such a nature as would sicken, rather than feast a civilized person. We shall forbear giving any details of their style of culinary, and be contented with saying that it was of such a character as not to admit of a description here.

At intervals along the valley might have been seen groups of Indians lounging lazily upon the grass, indulging in a game of hazard, or recounting to each other singular stories of their own heroic deeds. In every quarter a free social intercourse prevailed. The meeting appeared to be one of old friends, and each seemed anxious to relate his wonderful experience to the other. Feasting and conviviality prevailed everywhere in the broad valley; and with the bright sunlight dancing upon the troubled bosom of the rapids; with acres of curiously formed tents, and long rows of smouldering fires mingling their curling smokes; with thousands of strange, brawny Indian forms, painted and adorned, moving quickly to and fro—the scene was a curious and interesting blending of nature and savage pastime.

Muskets and war clubs, scalping-knives and tomahawks were laid aside, and each soul seemed, for the time being, to throw off every care of life, and to indulge his or her savage nature on the broadest principles of unrestrained, untrammelled freedom. Here the children of the forest once more enjoyed the pleasures of their annual feast, uninterrupted by any barrier of civilization. Only one white man's presence marred the curious harmony of the occasion. This was in the person of a French traveler and explorer, who, having skirted the western border of Lake Michigan, was now exploring the source of the Grand River. Arriving at this extensive but temporary settlement, he found the savages both friendly and hospitable, and accepted an invitation to mingle with them in some of the amusements of the occasion.

One phase of this broad, living picture was the sign of approaching danger to the eye of the French traveler. Not far from the tent of the principal chief lay five barrels of whisky, although at this stage of the proceedings not one had been opened.

Returning to the scene of action at the large tent spoken of at the beginning of this chapter, we find the heralds of the great chief busily engaged dragging, by means of rude wooden tongs, the hot stones from the embers of the three smouldering fires, and carrying them to a smaller tent, not more than twenty paces distant. The latter had been formed by twining together the tops of small trees, and covering them with blankets from top to bottom. In the center of this tent the Indians had dug out the earth, carefully removing it some distance, and were now filling the excavation with the hot stones, already mentioned. When this had been completed, three of the leading chiefs, after removing their scanty clothing, provided themselvss each with a sort of splint broom, and entered the small tent. Vessels of water were passed in and sprinkled upon the hot stones by the chiefs, who muttered a curious prayer as they waved the dripping brooms over the steaming mass.

This was called the exercise of purification, and must' indeed, have been a painful one to the three subjects within. This was kept up for nearly an hour, until the blankets which covered the tent were dripping with the evaporated steam. After the chiefs had been thoroughly steamed, and thereby purified, they came forth, their tawny skin presenting a par-boiled appearance, and passed into the large tent. Taking seats upon a small platform which had been erected at one end of the enclosure, and being provided with small red blankets with which to cover their nakedness, they busied themselves wiping the great drops of sweat from their bodies, while the principal young men and women who had come to the feast came in, in solemn procession, and occupied seats upon the circle of mats that had been carefully arranged for the purpose.

CHAPTER III.

ANNUAL ADDRESS OF THE CHIEFS—THE FEAST-DANCE —THE CAROUSE—SAVAGE INTOXICATION—THE END OF THE FEAST.

A SOLEMN silence prevailed. At length the oldest chief rose and began to recite the history of his tribe. He laid down the principles of their religion and government, and urged upon his young men the great importance of their duties. They should not only become acquainted with these things, but remember, support and honor them. They must perpetuate the principles of their religion, preserve the correct history of their tribe, and, at proper times, impress it upon the succeeding generation.

The two other purified chiefs followed with a similar address. When the last of these was concluded the assembled Indians prepared for their feast-dance, which was conducted in the same tent. This performance lasted about an hour, and was the most peculiar scene of the feast. The dance was conducted according to a system more complex, and, perhaps, more difficult to perform than any of those known to civilization. Yet each participant entered into it with an ease and grace truly admirable.

The only music was performed on a bark drum partly filled with corn, which, when beaten with a short stick, measured the time so accurately followed by the performers.

During the dance, some of the women, who took no part in the exercise, busied themselves in hiding the guns and other weapons, preparatory to the carouse which was to follow. At the conclusion of the exercises in the great tent the Indians repaired to the wigwam of their chief, where the whisky awaited their further action. The barrels were tapped and the liquid freely distributed among the thirsty savages, who soon became exceedingly happy. They kept up a continual drinking and shouting, and leaping, and performing all manner of acrobatic feats, until silenced in the sleep of intoxication. But during all this hilarity not a squaw tasted the liquor. They were, for the time being, contented with laughing at the curious feats of their drunken husbands or lovers. No sooner, however, had the joyous yells of the men subsided than the women began their indulgence, and the scene that followed is beyond all description. A drunken Indian cuts an amusing figure, but what shall we say of the intoxicated squaw ? She adds to his coarse jollity vulgar and mello-dramatic situations, from which the civilized eye turns away in horror and disgust.

But the women had their debauch with all its accompanying scenes of shameful induigences, and were soon prostrated among the senseless bodies of the men. Thus the scene changed. As evening drew near thousands of Indian forms lay motionless upon the green valley, while the mischievous children ran about leaping over them as if to act their part in the curious drama.

When darkness closed in upon the scene the stillness was broken only by the prattle of the children, with an occasional shout from some reviving savage, who, bewildered with the situation, seemed anxious to awaken his companions.

The night passed in comparative silence, and when the sun rose on the following morning, nearly all signs of intoxication had disappeared. The feast was continued several days, and not until serious differences began to arise among the Indians did they break up their time-honored exercises.

CHAPTER IV.

The Ottawa Mission—Unsuccessful Attempt of Mr. McCoy—Success of Rev. L. Slater—The Mission School—Some of its Characteristics.

From 1764 to 1820 the history of the Indian settlements in the vicinity of Grand Rapids is necessarily disconnected; yet, during most of this period, there were two or more permanent settlements on the west bank of the river—one of the Ottawas, and another of this nation and the Chippewas. The population of these villages varied with the seasons. In the spring and fall, the number of Indians collected here would often reach three or four thousand, but in mid-summer or winter it would sometimes be decreased to three or four hundred. Like all other Indian villages the inhabitants were a transient set, constantly moving away or returning, as their savage notions or the requirements of the chase demanded.

The village of the Ottawas was the most permanent, and, in point of population and influence, was the strongest settlement on the Grand River when the first rays of civilization broke through the forests from Detroit. Their rude huts were clustered along the western

margin of the rapids to the number of about one huu-
dred when Mr. Isaac McCoy visited the village in 1723,
for the purpose of establishing a station in the interests
of the government and civilization.

This gentleman, who resided at Fort Wayne, visited
Gen. Cass, at Detroit, in June, 1822, for the purpose of
securing the privileges of the Chicago treaty. The Gov-
ernor had already appointed a commissioner to make
definite arrangements with the Indians for the sites of
the missionary stations, and Grand Rapids had been
designated as a suitable place for the Ottawa Mission.
Mr. McCoy made the journey to this place in company
with a Frenchman, named Paget, in the following year.
On their arrival they met with so many difficulties that
they failed to accomplish their purpose. A council was
held with the Ottawa chiefs, and Mr. McCoy addressed
them through an interpreter, at considerable length, setting forth the plans of the government and the advantages which the Indians would derive from a cheerful acceptance of them. Kewaykushquom, chief of the Ottawa
village, replied in a brief speech, refusing to accept the
conditions offered.

In 1824, Rev. L. Slater, came to Grand Rapids, accompanied by a blacksmith and several workmen, and succeeded in winning the friendship of the savages. He
established the Baptist Mission, which afterwards performed efficient service in the interests of civilization.
The life of this christian pioneer was fraught with many
hardships; he began his work at Grand Rapids by erecting a log house for his own residence, and a log school
house. These were the first buildings ever erected by
civilized persons at Grand Rapids, although the Ameri-

can Fur Company had built a small store house about two miles farther up the river, as early as 1780.

Mr. Slater's labors were among the Ottawas, and he soon became a favorite with Chief Kewaykushquom. The little block school-house which had been erected under the auspices of his mission was soon filled with the children of the forest, where the light of christianity and civilization found its first admirers among the savages in the Grand River Valley.

At this point in our narrative, a mention of the events in commercial enterprise would seem necessary, but we shall follow out the record of the Baptist Mission, and at the beginning of the succeeding chapter, return to the scenes of the fur trade.

It is hardly necessary to say that Mr. Slater's efforts to convert and educate the savages were, like all other attempts of the kind, without satisfactory results; but while this end proved to be unattainable, the devoted missionary saw the fruits of his labors in another direction. If the Indian mind and heart could not appreciate and fully possess his religious doctrines, the christian influence which he brought to bear upon them so far subdued the savage nature as to give the votaries of

---

commercial enterprise a welcome among their villages. In this way Mr. Slater had his reward.

But his endeavors to convert the Ottawas were not wholly barren; nor were his labors to educate them without a degree of success. After laboring for some time in this rude building, a frame school house was erected, and the old block house converted into a dwelling. This modern mission school house was erected in 1837, by the same mission, and was situated near the corner of Bridge and Front streets. It was originally devoted to the Indian children attached to Mr. Slater's mission, but, owing to the influx of white population, and to the indisposition of the Indians, it was soon after appropriated to the former.

The first white school was opened in the spring of 1837, and Miss Bond, a young lady attached to the mission, installed as its first teacher. She taught one year beginning her labors with the following list of pupils: George and Emily Slater; Ezra, Samuel M., Selden E. and Alfred B. Turner; Mary and Sarah C. Sheldon; Aaron B., Alzina, Chester B., Clarissa and Thereosa Turner; Reuben E., Almira M,. and James N. Davis; Lucy Sliter; Cornelia and Henry W. Norton; Sally Willard

---

and Nathan Sibley; George M. and Clarissa White, and Arsnich, daughter of the Indian chief Mec-cis-si-nin-ni.

An old resident, writing of this school house, truthfully remarks: "It was not furnished with furnaces, wood ready sawed and a man to build fires. The caloric was generated by a huge sheet-iron box stove. Each patron of the school furnished so much wood per scholar, and as the wood was generally cut in sled lengths, the male portion of the scholars carried their axes and cut it into stove-wood at noon-time or recess. The 'Board of Education' was not pestered at that time for gymnastic apparatus for the purpose of giving the scholars an opportunity for exercising their muscle in order to give tone to their minds, for the teachers furnished all the apparatus necessary for that purpose, and, I may add, applied it with severity."

The school, in those days commenced at 8 o'clock A. M. and closed at 5 P. M., and was kept open six days in the week. Nothing was considered a sufficient excuse for dismissing school save the celebration of the "Glorious Fourth."

The inside of the house was not furnished with patent desks and seats, but with benches, some of which were

---

made of planed boards, and others of unplaned slabs, flat side up, with pegs for legs. There were two desks for writing, extending the length of the sides of the building. When the hour for writing arrived the scholars were directed to face the wall. This afforded an excellent chance for the teacher to look over the shoulder of the pupil, see how the quill pen was held, and when the marks were too horizontal and perpendicular. If either were the case, "a reminder" was put in, the position of the scholar affording too good an opportunity to be lightly thrown away. The result of this "correction" would be the making of sundry lines and curves unknown in geometry.

It was the custom in those days to hold evening "spelling school" about twice in every week. There was a larger attendance at this than at the regular day school. The exercises usually closed with the scholars standing up and "spelling down," and the contest was usually attended with considerable excitement.

CHAPTER V.

INCIDENTS OF EARLY SETTLEMENT—ARRIVAL OF LOUIS CAMPAU—HONESTY OF THE INDIANS—THE DEXTER COLONY—THE FIRST POSTMASTER—INCIDENTS OF LETTER WRITING.

MR. SLATER'S christian labors having let a ray of light into the wilderness, commerce, her necessary handmaid, was not long in following. Louis Campau was the first white person who came to Grand Rapids to build himself a home. He was born in Detroit in the year 1791. His ancestors were French, and came to Detroit before the war of the Revolution. He had not the advantages of early education, but, being endowed with a clear intellect and great force of character, he became a useful and valued citizen.

He came to Grand Rapids at the solicitation, and under the patronage of Mr. William Brewster, of Detroit, who was extensively engaged in the fur business, in rivalry with the American Fur Company, and who furnished him with all that was required to successfully prosecute the business. Mr. Campau afterward opened trading posts and established his agents at Muskegon,

---

Manistee, Kalamazoo, Lowell, Hastings and Eaton Rapids. All the Indians with whom he came in contact were both friendly and peaceful. They were also honest, and could be trusted with goods, never even in a single instance failing to pay as soon as they had the ability. Fur was the principal currency of that day, and the Indians found a lucrative business in exchanging it for the products of civilization.

For more than seven years Mr. Campau's only white companions were traders like himself, with an occasional traveler. He made but a faint attempt at improving the place, having cleared away only about three acres of timber during the first five years of his residence in this place. But in 1833 the pioneers of civilization began to arrive. A land office was opened at White Pigeon and Mr. Campau and Mr. Luther Lincoln were the first purchasers. Mr. Lincoln's purchase included the site of the present village of Grandville, and that of Mr. Campau comprised a tract in which a portion of the city of Grand Rapids is now located.

In the spring of 1833, Mr. Samuel Dexter came to Ionia with a colony of sixty-three persons from New York, cutting a road through the woods from Pontiac,

---

which was afterwards known as the Dexter Trail.   Mr.
Dexter afterwards laid out what is known as the Dexter
Fraction of Grand Rapids.   Most of the colonists accompanying this gentleman became residents of this city
and succeeded in establishing themselves in the best business interests of the city.

This was the beginning of settlement, and it was continued with increasing numbers.   Following Mr. Dexter,
came Mr. Joel Guild, who purchased the lot from Mr.
Campau, on which the City National Bank now stands,
paying the small sum of twenty-five dollars therefor.
On the following summer he erected a small frame house
on his lot which was the second building put up on the
west side of the river.   Mr. Guild brought with him his
family consisting of a wife and seven children.   He soon
became honorably identified with the early enterprise
of Grand Rapids, and lived to see his sons and daughters comfortably settled.   Soon after his arrival he was
appointed Postmaster and held the position for several
years, or until succeeded by Darius Windsor.

While Mr. Guild was Postmaster of Grand Rapids the
mail was brought to the city once a month on the backs
of Indian ponies. The postage on a single letter was two

---

shillings, and, during the first two or three years times were so hard among the settlers that the poorer class found it a difficult matter to raise funds for a regular correspondence. Many a true hearted pioneer carried his carefully folded letter, sealed with red wax, in his "waist-coat" pocket, waiting and longing for something to turn up by which he might raise the coveted shilling for the necessary postage, while, perhaps, his "sweet heart," anxiously waiting the arrival of the same missive in some eastern home, her troubled heart filled with unpleasant forebodings of inconstancy. But these early settlers were not easily discouraged. Many of them worked a whole week for one shilling rather than to give their intended partners cause for doubt, and cheerfully gave the six days hard earnings, no doubt in the belief that when the letter reached its owner its true value would be fully appreciated. I have been told of one instance in which the pioneer's heart became so wrought up from being unable to pay the postage on a love-letter which he had carried in his pocket four months, that he gave a new pair of boots for the required shilling. That letter, which I was permitted to read, only a few days ago at the house of one of the oldest residents in Grand Rapids contains the following paragraph:

"Dear Jane: I reckon you have gone off and married another man, and if you havn't already I'm afraid you will before this reaches you, for, at the present time, I have no money to pay the postage with, and can see no way to get it. We are having hard times here this winter. The flour is all gone and we have no money, but I am still true to my last promise, and trust you will wait until I can make it good."

This fearful heart was afterwards cheered by the arrival of "Jane," who became his wife at Grand Rapids in 1839.

This case has many parallels in the early history of the city, but those times have thoroughly passed away, and now almost any quantity of love may be sent abroad for three cents.

In 1833 there were only a few acres of cleared land on either side of the rapids. The Indians had several acres cleared on the west side just below where the railroad bridge now crosses the river. Here was located the village of the Ottawas, containing about sixty huts, and, perhaps, three hundred inhabitants. It was among these Indians that the Rev. Mr. Slater established the mission spoken of in the previous chapter. The chief of the village was called Kewaykushquom, who, besides ruling

---

these savages, held a limited sway over the village of the
Ottawas and Chippewas, located about half a mile further
up the river, on the same side. The subordinate chief
of the latter village was called Noonday.

It was at this village that the Catholic Mission was
established.

Many of the old settlers of Grand Rapids are unable
to give any account of this village, and some of them dispute the fact of its existence there at this period. This
may be accounted for, as it was a transient settlement,
and at an early day became united with the Ottawas under Kewaykushquom, a few scattering families of the
Chippewas only remaining to perpetuate their government. These soon became unwelcome intruders in the
eyes of the Ottawas, and were either driven away or
forced to join them.

Besides this permanent Indian settlement there was
always a large number of the Ottawas and Chippewas,
who, returning from the chase, would gather upon the
western bank of the rapids every spring and fall. These
semi-annual encampments became larger and of greater
importance after the government adopted its system of
distributing clothing and other necessaries to the Indians in this vicinity.

We shall now pass on with the incidents of early settlement, and again return to a more detailed description of these villages.

CHAPTER VI.

EARLY SETTLERS—THE CATHOLIC MISSION—DISPUTE BETWEEN MR. CAMPAU AND FATHER BARRIGAU—THE DARK DAYS OF KENT—INCREASE OF IMIGRATION—COURTSHIPS—THE FIRST MARRIAGE—THE FIRST TOWN MEETING—BUILDINGS—THE PIONEER LAWYER AND DOCTOR—RE-ESTABLISHMENT OF THE CATHOLIC MISSION—SUCCESS OF REV. FATHER VOZOISKY.

THE tide of emigration had now fairly set in, and in a few years Grand Rapids became quite a village.

Mr. E. Turner and Mr. Ira Jones came in 1833, and also, during the same year, Mr. Jonathan F. Chubb, with his family. Mr. Chubb located and cultivated a farm between Grand Rapids and Grandville, but after devoting only a few years to this work he sold his farm, moved into the city and opened an agricultural store on Canal street. He died several years ago, and his son, A. L. Chubb, succeeds him in active business life.

It was at this period that the Catholic mission, already spoken of, was established. The Baptist mission was then in full operation among the Ottawas under Keway-kushquom, therefore the Rev. Father Barrigau chose Noonday's village for the site of his mission house. This priest began his labors in 1833, and in the latter part of the same year erected a small frame building on the outskirts of this village. Mr. Louis Campau wanted the building on the east side of the river and eventually carried his point, and engaged a man named Barney

Burton to move it across the river on the ice. Rev. Father Barrigau did not suit the singular, and to some extent, impracticable notions of Mr. Campau, and soon left in consequence. Thus the Catholic mission died out for the time.

During this period, when Mr. Campau and Mr. Barrigau were disagreeing over certain religious matters, which resulted in breaking up the Catholic school, the children on the east side of the river were taken across to Rev. Mr. Slater's mission school in a birch-bark canoe, returning by the same means in the evening.

These were dark days in the history of Grand Rapids. Only a few pioneers, not to exceed thirty, then struggled for an existence here. Most of them had come for the purpose of trading with the Indians, and took but little interest in the improvement of the place ; while, on the other hand, there were a few enterprising, far-sighted Americans among them, who, foreseeing the future greatness of the site, began to clear away the forests with a view to erecting a permanent home. These persons, no doubt, appeared somewhat enthusiastic in the eyes of the French traders, who have never been able to see anything in the future of Michigan until it has been fully accomplished; but some of these persons still live to feel and realize vastly more than these "enthusiastic pioneers" ever hoped for.

One day, during the winter of 1834-5, an American who had purchased a small lot remarked to Mr. Campau that he believed Grand Rapids, then the obscure hamlet of Kent, would, in less than twenty years, become a flourishing city. The good old pioneer and father of the city responded with a sneer, for at this time he could see nothing in Grand Rapids beyond the fur trade. But even this patriarch has lived to feel the power and see the matchless results of American enterprise. He has lived to see his forest trading post converted into a great manufacturing and commercial mart. He sought a home in the forest, but lived to see that home surrounded by a populous city, and died in the midst of civilization.

In 1834 the tide of emigration rolled along with steady progress. Among the most notable who came were Richard Godfroy, Robert Barrs, Louis Morau and Lovell Moore. This year is notable for one single event—the first marriage in Grand Rapids. The happy pair were Harriet Guild and Barney Burton. The courtship was conducted here beside the old-fashioned fire-place, in the little house of Mr. Joel Guild, which stood where the City National Bank now stands. Barney was a hard working fellow, steady, honest and genial, and many a long evening did he entertain Harriet with curious pictures of their future home and happiness. She listened with increasing interest, perhaps forgetting that the hour was growing late; for in those days getting married was almost always prefaced by a hearty courtship—a courtship not of afternoon calls, in which the aspirant for matrimonial blessings is entertained with piano music, but a courtship extending into the solemn stillness of the night, when, by the dim firelight, which revealed the honest faces of only two at every glare, the vows were made—vows seldom broken. Such was Barney Burton's courtship. Returning from the woods, after a hard day's work of "saw-logging," he would carefully lay aside his buck-skin moccasins, and, putting on his "Sunday clothes," he would skip over to Uncle Joel's, where he always found the true-hearted Harriet to welcome him. Such pastimes, I fancy, caused Barney to forget his weariness, and to think only of happier days to come.

It was also in 1834 that the first town meeting was held, and this, too, was held at Mr. Guild's residence, which was, at this period, the principal frame building in the settlement of Kent. There were only nine voters. The township was organized on the 4th of April in this year. There does not appear to have been any defined limits to the organization, but it is supposed to have embraced all the settlements within the present county of

Kent. The division now known as the township of Grand Rapids, received its name in 1842.

As I have already said, the first township meeting was held in the house of Joel Guild, and the number of electors was nine. The officers elected were: Rix Robinson, Supervisor; E. Turner, Clerk; Joel Guild and Barney Burton, Assessors; Ira Jones, Collector. At the time of the organization and for several years thereafter, the taxes were collected by the Collector, and paid over to the Supervisor, and disbursed by him. The first Treasurer was elected in 1839, aud the first entry upon his books was as follows: "May 14th, 1839.—Received of E. W. Davis, Supervisor, eight dollars on the Grand River Bank; three dollars on the Ypsilanti Bank; one dollar and twenty-five cents on the Pontiac Bank, and sixty-two cents in specie." The amount of taxes that had been collected the year previous was $174. This includes all the taxes collected in 1838 in the whole county of Kent. From this statement the rapid growth of the city and county is apparent to all.

Among the settlers of 1834 were Ezekiel Davis, Lewis

Reed, Ezra Reed, Porter Reed, David S. Leavitt, and Robert M. Barr. Among those who followed in 1835-6-7 were James McGrath, George Young, Robert Thompson, John W. Fisk, Matthew Taylor, Leonard Covell, John F. Godfroy, James Nelson, and a host of others, who have since made comfortable homes for themselves in or around the city of Grand Rapids.

The first hotel put up in Kent was erected by Mr. Fisk, and was afterwards known as the Lake House.

In the fall of 1834 Mr. Louis Campau commenced a large frame building, which, to this day, exists as the upper two stories of a part of the Rathbun House, and in the following year there was a general movement of settlers from various parts of northwestern Michigan and from Detroit to Grand Rapids. Among these were Edward Guild and Darius Winsor, from Ionia; Hon. Lucius Lyon, Jefferson Morrison, Antoine Campau, James Lyman, A. Hosford Smith, D. Turner, W. C. Godfroy, Dr. Wilson, Dr. Charles Shepard, and Julius C. Abel. Dr. Wilson was the first doctor in Kent. He was furnished with a medicine case and a set of instruments by

Louis Campau, and commenced practicing in Grand Rapids in the fall of 1835, when the total white population of the village was not more than fifty.

Julius C. Abel was the pioneer lawyer, and soon became rich out of the misunderstandings and legal conflicts of the inhabitants. James Lyman and Jefferson Morrison put up stores and commenced trading. These improvements or additions to the little town were valuable aids, for, at this period, commerce seems to have got a legitimate foothold in the place.

In the same year Mr. N. O. Sargeant, purchased an interest with Lucius Lyon in the Kent Plat, and came on with a large number of workmen for the purpose of digging a mill-race. Judge Almy and wife came at the same time.

The entrance of Mr. Sargeant's expedition was indeed an exciting event in the little town of Kent. The workmen came into the place with their shovels and picks on their shoulders, marching in double file, to the inspiriting notes of a bugle in the hands of one of their number. The chief of the Ottawa village beheld the demon-

---

stration with amazement and immediately despatched one of his deputies to Mr. Campau, with offers of assistance to help me drive the invaders, as he regarded them, from the town. The chief was so far excited by this entry of pioneers that he assembled his warriors in council so as to be ready for action as soon as the deputy returned from Mr. Campau. The reader will scarcely be able to imagine the chargrin of these disappointed indians when the deputy returned and announced Mr. Campau's reply in the following words: "These are our friends and brethern who have come to labor with us, let us welcome them!"

Among the prominent arrivals in 1835 was the Rev. Father Vizoisky, who was for seventeen years, pastor of the Catholic flock in Grand Rapids. This good man was a native of Hungary, and received his education at the Catholic institutions of learning in Austria under the patronage of the Hungarian Chancery. He came to the United States in 1831. By the appointment of the Bishop of Detroit he officiated three years in St. Clair county, and in 1835, he removed to the Grand River Mission which had been broken up in the manner already described. Among the other settlers of 1835, I will also mention Lyman and Horace Gray, Andrew Robbins, Martin Ryerson.

The Rev. Father Vizoisky's ministry in Grand Rapids was marked by unsurpassed devotion, and the most gratifying success. No road was rough enough and no weather inclement enough to keep him from the post of duty. To the poor he brought relief; to the sick consolation; and to the dying the absalvatory promises of his office. He died January 2d, 1852, at the age of sixty years; having lived to see a handsome stone chuch edifice erected on Monroe St. two years previous to his death, and filled with a numerous and prosperous congregation.

CHAPTER VII.

The Mania of Speculation—New Settlers—Fictitious Values—Wild-cat Money—Hard Times—Ruin of the Banks—A Bleak and Dreary Winter—The Hard Flour—A Welcome Spring—More Emigrants.

In 1836 the mania of speculation, which pervaded all Michigan, found many enthusiastic votaries in the town of Kent. Lots were held at almost as high prices as they will bring to-day. If a man bought a piece of land for $100, he at once set his price at $1,000, and confidently awaited a purchaser. The currency was inflated and "wild-cat money" in superabundance supported these fictitious values. Everybody got largely in debt, and for the time being, became intoxicated with a fiction, but all lived to repent their extravagance, long and bitterly.

We have no space here to give a list of the emigrants of 1836, but among the most important were Hon. John Ball, William A. Richmond, John W. Pierce, P. Tracy, E. W. Barnes, Isaac Turner, A. B. Turner, George C. Nelson, James M. Nelson, Warren P. Mills, George Young, Robert Hilton, B. Stocking, Abram Randall, T. H. Lyon, William Haldane, L. M. Page, C. H. Taylor, Jacob Barnes, William Morman, David Burnett, K. S. Pettibone, E. Davis, Samuel Howland, J. M. Smith, H. Green, Geo. Coggeshall, J. J. Watson, Geo. Martin, Myron Hinsdill, Stephen Hinsdill, Hiram Hinsdill, and Harry Eaton. Mr. Eaton, in 1840, was elected Sheriff of the county.

The parts acted by these several gentlemen in building up the city may be briefly summed up as follows:

Hon. John Ball came here to speculate in lands, and, although having been educated as a lawyer, has since devoted more of his time to real estate business than to the practice of law. He took A. D. Rathbun into part-

---

nership in 1840, who continued in the same relation for about one year. In 1844, S. L. Withey became his partner, and the firm was then known as Ball & Withey. Afterwards George Martin became a partner, and the firm was Ball, Martin & Withey. Again, it was Ball, Withey & Sargeant, and it is now Ball & McKee. Mr. Ball has taken an active part in the affairs of the town and city since his first residence here. In 1838 he represented this district in the State Legislature, and was an able member of that body. He has also been honorably identified with the public schools of Grand Rapids, and has, in every instance, acted for the best interests of the growing city.

Myron Hinsdill erected the National Hotel in 1836, which soon after went into the hands of Canton Smith, and was successfully conducted by him for several years.

John W. Pierce, the pioneer dry goods man of Kent, came to Grand Rapids with Judge Almy, and assisted that gentleman in surveying a portion of the city. He erected a dwelling on Ottawa street in 1842, and resided in it until 1870, when he removed to his new and elegant residence on the corner of Bronson and Kent streets, having occupied his old mansion for nearly twenty-seven years. Mr. Pierce was among that number who, in the darkest days, had an abiding faith in the future growth of Kent, and by his great perseverence, energy and integrity, he has accumulated considerable wealth for himself, and added not a little to the growth and development of the city. On his arrival in Grand Rapids there were only thirteen frame buildings in the town, and his book store was the first one established in Michigan outside of Detroit.

John J. Watson came from Detroit, and in 1836 erected a very large store-house. It was afterwards moved up the river, and became a part of Hon. W. D. Foster's old wooden store.

George Martin, previously mentioned among 1836 settlers, was a graduate of Middlebury College, Vt. He was, for a number of years, County and Circuit Judge of this county, and at the time of his death, was Chief Justice of the Supreme Court of Michigan.

In 1836 Richard Godfroy built the first steamboat on Grand River, and called it the "Gov. Mason." The first boat, however, other than the batteaux of the traders, was a pole boat called the "Young Napoleon," con structed for Mr. Campau by Lyman Gray. The "Gov. Mason" was con nanded by Captain Stoddard. It was wrecked off the mouth of the Muskegon River in 1838.

In our list of the pioneers of 1836 we have mentioned Judge Almy. He was a civil engineer and practical surveyor of considerable eminence, and was in charge, in 1837–8, of the Grand and Kalamazoo rivers ; was a member of the State Legislature, and one of the County

Judges. He was a lawyer by profession, but did not, for some reason, practice any after coming to Michigan.

George Coggeshall came from Wilmington, N. C., with his family and invested his means in Kent property. He erected a frame house on the corner of Bridge and Kent streets, and proved a valuable citizen of the town.

Among the pioneers of 1837 were I. V. Harris, Rev. James Ballard, Leonard Covell, G. M. McGray, William A. Lyon, L. R. Atwater, William I. Blakely, A. Dikeman, H. K. Rose, John F. Godfroy, Gains S. Deane, Henry Deane, C. P. Calkins and Col. S. F. Butler.

The first bank established in the town was the Grand River Bank, established in 1837. Judge Almy was its first President, and Hon. Lucius Lyon cashier. It existed two years, and finally went down under the weight of hard times and left its notes a complete loss in the hands of the unfortunate holders.

The People's Bank was started in the same year under the management of George Coggeshall, with Louis Campau as President and Simeon Johnson as cashier. This institution failed to comply with the State laws and was

---

soon wound up, Hon. John Ball being appointed receiver.

For two or three years succeeding this the town of Kent was one of the "bluest" places in all Michigan. Times were hard beyond all description. Lots of real estate that had been sold for $1,000 a year or six months previous would not bring $100 now. Indeed, they were hardly worth the taxes, and in some instances lots were sacrificed to accomplish this and this only. Nearly all the mechanics who had been attracted here by the rapid growth of the place were thrown out of employment and left in disgust. Everybody became disheartened, and during the winther of 1837–8 nearly all would have left could they have sold their property for a quarter of its value.

It was during this winter that the supplies became short. A schooner, loaded with flour and bound for the Grand River, was caught in a storm at the head of Lake Michigan, and leaked so badly that all her cargo became wet. However, after a long and dangerous voyage she arrived at the mouth of Grand River and her cargo of

---

flour was brought up the river to the town of Kent.
When the barrels were opened the flour was found to
have been wet, and in consequence it was caked so hard
as to require an axe or hatchet to break it. This was
the only flour that could be obtained during the long
winter, and even this was sold as high as twenty-two
dollars a barrel. Before it could he made into bread it
was pounded up like so much plaster, and after being
powdered fine, was quite novel in appearance, having
adopted the color of lake water, instead of that of pure
flour. The bread produced from it was eaten because
there was no choice in the matter, except to eat it or
none.

The winter was, indeed, a hard one. Sickness prevailed largely, and hunger and distress was shockingly
abundant. The Indians, who had been accustomed to
receive food and clothing from the whites, were now left
to their own limited resources, and many of them perished during the long cold winter. It was not much better among the white population. The winter was endured, not enjoyed; and when the genial spring of '38

---

drew near, its warmth was greeted with peculiar gratitude by the half-perishing settlers of Grand Rapids. But as soon as navigation opened the supplies increased and times were slightly improved.

Among the settlers of this year I will mention W. D. Roberts, John T. Holmes, Amos Roberts, C. W. Taylor, Erastus Clark, J. T. Finney and Solomon Withey and his sons.

I should have mentioned that the Bridge Street House was erected in 1837, and opened by John Thompson; subsequently it was kept by Solomon Withey, who was succeeded by W. A. Tryon and T. H. Lyon.

CHAPTER VIII.

The First Newspaper in Grand Rapids—Some Difficulties in Procuring a Press—A Review of Grand Rapids in 1837—Editorial Predictions.

In 1837, we have to notice several important events. The first newspaper ever printed in Grand Rapids was established in this year. It was called the Grand Rapids *Times*, and was started by George N. Pattison, the first number being issued on the 18th of April.

Several copies of the first number are still extant, having been printed on cloth with a view to their preservation.

Mr. Pattison was assisted in the editorial work by Mr. Noble H. Finney.

The press on which this paper was printed was drawn up the river from Grand Haven, on the ice by a team of dogs. It was purchased the winter previous at Buffalo, by Judge Almy. At Detroit it was shipped for Grand Haven on the steamer Don Quixote which was wrecked off Thunder Bay, and the press taken around the lakes on another boat.

The first number of the *Times* contained the following article on Grand Rapids: Though young in its improvements, the site of this village has long been known, and esteemed for its natural advantages. It was here that the Indian traders long since made their grand depot. It was at this point that the missionary herald established his institution of learning—taught the forest child the beauties of civilization and inestimable benefits of the christian religion. This has been the choicest, dearest spot to the unfortunate Indians and won the pride of the white man. Like other villages of the west, its transition from the savage to a civilized state has been as sudden as its prospects are now flattering.

Who would have believed to have visited this place two years since, (1835) when it was inhabited only by a few families, most of whom were of French origin, a people so eminent for exploring the wilds and meandering rivers of the west that this place would now contain its twelve hundred inhabitants. Who would have imag-

---

ined that thus rapid would have been the improvement of this romantic place. The rapidity of its settlement is beyond the most visionary anticipation; but its location, its advantage and its clime, were sufficient to satisfy the observing mind that nothing but the frown of Proidence could blast its prospects.

The river upon which this town is situated is one of the most important and delightful to be found in the county—not important and beautiful alone for its clear, silver-like water, winding its way through a romantic valley of some hundred miles, but for its width and depth, its susceptibility for steam navigation, and the immense hydraulic power afforded at this point.

We feel deeply indebted to our Milwaukee friends for their lucid description of the advantages to be derived from a connection of the waters of this river with those of Detroit, by canal or railroad. A canal is nearly completed around the rapids at this place, sufficiently large to admit boats to pass up and down, with but litttle detention. Several steamboats are now preparing to commence regular trips from Lyons, at the mouth of the

Maple River to this place, a distance of sixty miles; and from this to Grand Haven, a distance of thirty-five miles, thence to Milwaukee and Chicago.

Thus the village of Grand Rapids, with a navigable stream, a water-power of twenty-five feet fall, an abundance of crude building material, stone of excellent quality, pine, oak and other timber in immense quantities within its vicinity, can but flourish—can but be the Rochester of Michigan! The basement story of an extensive mill, one hundred and sixty by forty feet, is now completed; a part of the extensive machinery is soon to be put in operation. There are now several dry goods and grocery stores, some three or four public houses, one large church, erected, and soon to be finished in good style, upon the expense of a single individual, who commenced business a few years ago by a small traffic with the Indians. Such is the encouragement to western pioneers! The village plat is upon the bold bank of a river, extending back upon an irregular plain some eighty to a hundred rods to rising bluffs, from the base and sides of which some of the most pure, crystal-like fountains of water burst out in boiling springs, pouring forth streams that murmur over their pebbly bottoms, at once a delight to the eye and an invaluable luxury to the thirsty palate.

New England may surpass this place with her lofty mountains, but not with her greatest boast, purity and clearness of water. Our soil is sandy and mostly dry. The town is delightful, whether you view it from the plains upon the banks of the river, or from the bluffs that overlook the whole surrounding country. To ascend these bluffs you take a gradual rise to the height of a hundred feet, when the horizon only limits the extent of vision. The scenery, to an admirer of beautiful land-scape, is truly picturesque and romantic. Back, east of the town, is seen a widespread plain of burr oak, at once easy to cultivate and inviting to the agriculturist. Turning westward, especially at the setting of the sun, you behold the most enchanting prospect; the din of the ville below, the broad sheet of water murmuring over the rapids, the sunbeams dancing upon its swift gliding ripples, the glassy river at last losing itself in its distant meandering, presents a scenery that awakens the most lively emotions. But the opposite shore, upon which you behold a rich, fertile plain, still claims no small amount of admiration. Near the bank of the river is seen the little rude village of the more civilized Indians —their uncouth frame dwellings, the little churches and mound like burrying places. The number and size of the mounds, which mark the place where lies the remains of the proud warrior and the more humble of his un-tamed tribe, too plainly tell the endearments of that lovely plain to the native aborigines. And how quick the mind would follow the train of association to by-gone days and contrast these reflections with present appearances. Thus we see the scenes of savage life quickly spread upon the broad canvass of imagination. The proud chieftain seated and his tribe surrounding the council fires, the merry war dance, the wild amusements of the red man of the forest, and as soon think of their present unhappy condition. The bright flame of their lighted piles has been extinguished, and with it has faded the keen, expressive brilliancy of the wild man's eye. Their lovely Owashtenong, upon which their light canoes have so long glided, is now almost deserted.

It is from this point, too, that you can see in the distance the ever green tops of the lofty pines waving in majesty above the sturdy oak, the beech and maple, presenting to the eye the wild, undulating plain, with its thousand charms. Such is the location, the beauty and the advantages of this youthful town. The citizens are of the most intelligent, enterprising and industrious character. Their buildings are large, tasty and handsomely furnished. The clatter of mallet and chisel, the

---

clink of the hammer, the many newly raised and recently covered frames, and the few skeleton boats upon the wharves of the river, speak loudly for the enterprise of the place.   Mechanics of all kinds find abundance of employment, and reap a rich reward for their labor. Village property increases in value, and the prospect of wealth is alike flattering to all. What the sequel of such advantages and prospects will be, time alone must determine.

But a view of this place and its vicinity, where we find a rich and fertile soil, watered with the best of springs, and enjoying, as we do, a solubrious climate, a healthy atmosphere and the choicest gifts of a benign Benefactor, would satisfy almost anyone that this will soon be a bright star in the constellation of western villages.

We are now able to realize to what extent the predictions or anticipations of this article were well founded. Grand Rapids has not only become a bright star in the constellation of western villages, but in the constellation of western cities, and is the second city in population and importance in the prosperous State of Michigan.

CHAPTER IX.

The First White Pioneer—Her Operations with the Savages—The Indian Villages—Fate of Kewaykushquom—The Treaty—Indian Dissatisfaction.

I will now go back and notice the Grand Rapids Indians in the last days of their settlements.

As early as 1780 we find two flourishing Indian villages

located on the western bank of the Grand River, about midway of the rapids. They were about a quarter of a mile apart, and were under the government of two separate chiefs and councils; although the one was, to a small degree, subordinate to the other.

The larger of these contained about seven hundred inhabitants of the Ottawa and Chippewa natives, and was governed by the far-sighted and cunning Kewaykushquom, a chief of considerable renown; while the smaller did not contain more than five hundred souls, mostly Ottawas, and recognized Noonday as their chief.

At this time, all the land east of the Grand River, or the Owoshtenong, was owned by the Ottawas; and that west of the river was the joint property of that nation and the Chippewas.

The habits and customs of these savages differed in no essential point from those in other sections. They were industrious, honest and peaceful tribes, enjoying the advantages of the fur trade, and indulging all the curious customs characteristic of their race. The American Fur Company had, at this time, established a trading post about two miles below the present town of Lowell, on the Grand River, where their agent, Mrs. La Framboie, exchanged the products of civilization for peltries.

It will surprise the reader to learn that a woman was the first pioneer of civilization who ever set foot upon the pleasant valley of Grand River; but such, indeed, is the truth. She was a French lady of more than ordinary force of character, a shrewd trader and a bold adventurer. Her life at this outpost is filled with thrilling incidents, many of which are enlivened by a vein of romance.

Although the American Fur Company constantly kept a supply of goods at this point, the Indians would often go to Detroit to trade, not so much, however, with a view to securing larger prices for their peltries, or to purchasing necessaries at a smaller cost, as to obtain a supply of *fire-water*, which could not be had at a nearer point. As the time for the "annual pow-wow" approached, a journey to Detroit was considered necessary, for the purpose of laying in a supply of rum for the occasion.

Mrs. La Framboie remained at this post until superceded by Rix Robinson, in 1821. She had been a successful agent for the company, but her advanced age and the growing interests of the fur trade demanded her removal. Remnants of the old store-house in which she transacted business with the savages still remain. There is a part of the chimney yet standing, and marks of the excavations in which the canoes were hid may be seen near by. These are the oldest relics of pioneer life in Kent county.

Kewaykushquom, the great Chief of the Grand Rapids Indians, was prevailed upon in 1835 to enter into a treaty with the United States Government ceding all the lands west of Grand river.

To accomplish this treaty he made a journey to Washington in company with Rix Robinson and others, where he was entertained by the President, who made him many presents and won his warmest friendship.

By the stipulations of this treaty all the Indians in the vicinity of Owashtenong were to remove to a reservation west of the Mississippi.

When Kewaykushquom returned and laid the plan of the treaty before a council of the chiefs of the villages it was received with great disapproval. Many of the savage councilmen delivered long and eloquent speeches setting forth the disadvantage of leaving their homes which had become dear to Indian hearts by many fond recollections. "Here we have buried our dead," said one of the chiefs, "and here we should remain to protect their graves. This is our home—the home of our youth. Here we were reared on the banks of the beloved Owashtenong whose beauty has become our pride and boast.

Here our fathers died and were laid to rest. Here we have held our councils, prosecuted our trade, and preserved peace and friendship with all nations. Why go to a strange land to mingle with strange people, why forsake the graves of our ancestors? Have we become unpleasant to our brothers the whites that we must hide ourselves from their presence. What evil have we committed? Why thus sacrifice that which is most dear to the heart of every Chief and warrior. Has our Chief tasted the *fire water* of the pale faces and been blinded to the welfare of his people? Let him answer!"

Kewaykusquom replied in an eloquent speech, representing the advantages of the treaty and urging his subjects to extend a cheerful acquiescence, but to all his pleadings he received a prompt and indignant rebuke. They claimed that he had sold their homes and their liberties and had therefore become their enemy.

This council was held in 1835, at the village of the Ottawas and Chippewas, on the west side of the river, and resulted in the ruin of Kewaykushquom.

From that day he was pursued by his enemies until he

---

was cruelly murdered in his miserable tent, at the bend
of the river, in 1846. He had been deprived of the
honors and power of his official station; and after wan-
dering in distress for many years, and becoming bur-
dened with the weight of old age, he committed himself
to the care of two of his grandchildren. His lodge was
located only a short distance from Grand Rapids, and
many a white man and woman visited his tent to admin
ister relief to the sick and suffering Chief.

One Sabbath morning when Kewaykushquom lay
helpless and suffering upon his rude couch attended by
his devoted grandchildren, he was called upon by one
of the principal residents of Grand Rapids, who brought
with him some refreshments. The Chief was too sick
to partake of them. The man remarked to him that his
journey was nearly ended, and his reply was, "I am going
to leave this country for a land where the pursuit of my
enemies can torment me no more."

The next day an Indian entered his tent and requested the squaw who was attending Kewaykushquom to go
out and get a pail of water. She complied, leaving him

---

alone with the Chief. He then drew a knife from his bosom and thrust it into the heart of the helpless Indian. Having thus satisfied his savage heart with the vengeance that had haunted Kewaykushquom for nearly ten years, he made his escape. When the squaw returned with the water, she found her patient struggling in the agonies of death.

Meccissininni succeeded Kewaykushquom as a Chief of the Ottawa village. He also entered into a treaty for the sale of the lands on which the village was located, but was more successful than his predecessor in securing the hearty cooperation of his subjects.

He was an eloquent orator, a very proud, haughty Indian, and manifested a strong desire to secure an education. He always dressed like a white man. He was one of the chiefs who accompanied Louis Campau, Rix Rob_ inson and Rev. Mr. Slater to Washington to make a treaty relative to selling their lands, in 1335. This was the same treaty which caused the ruin, and, finally, the murder of Kewaykushquom. While in Washington, President Jackson wished to make Meccissininni a present of a new suit of clothes, and asked him what kind he would prefer. He said, as General Jackson was chief of his people, and he was chief of the red men, he thought it would be appropriate if he had a suit like his. The President ordered the suit. It was a black frock coat, black satin vest, black pantaloons, silk stockings, and pumps; but the best of the affair was, Gen. Jackson wore, at that time, a white bell-crowned hat, with a weed on it, being in mourning for his wife. The unsuspecting Indian, not knowing that the weed was a badge of mourning, had one on his hat, also, which pleased the

President and his Cabinet not a little. The chief was much delighted with the warm reception he received in the different cities on his return home.

After he returned a council met to hear the nature of the treaty, when Meccissininni distinguished himself as an orator in his portrayal of the treaty. He sold their lands, and the treaty provided for their removal west of the Mississippi in a certain number of years.

The chiefs and councilmen were opposed to the treaty and spoke violently against it, but this cunning Indian won them over to a reluctant acceptance of it. He said that for himself he would rather remain here, and be buried where his forefathers were; but on his people's account he had rather go west of the Mississippi, as his people would become debased by their association with the pale-faces.

Meccissininni distinguished himself among the Grand Rapids Indians as well as among the white inhabitants, for his generosity, gentlemanly bearing, great foresight and capacious intellect. He was, as far as possible, a civilized red man, and appeared to appreciate civilization to a very high degree.

In 1841 he was invited to a Fourth of July celebration. The dinner was served up near the site of Ball's foundry, where, after the oration and refreshments, the cloth was removed and regular toasts drank. Meccissininni was called upon for a toast, and responded as follows: "The pale faces and the red men—the former a great nation, and the latter a remnant of a great people; may they ever meet in unity together, and celebrate this great day as a band of brothers."

At one time this chief wanted to get trusted for some provisions and said he would pay at the next Indian payment. When he returned from the annual payment he was asked to settle his bill. He told the dealer to put it on paper and send it to his house and he would pay it, and remarked further, that he wished to do business like white people. So the dealer made out his bill, repaired to the chief's house, and was ushered in with all the politeness imaginable. He promptly paid the bill, and signified his wish to have it receipted.

About the year 1843, he was attacked with a disease which, after a short illness, terminated his existence, at

---

the age of fifty years. He lived and died a professor of the Catholic faith, under the spiritual guidance of the Rev. Father Vizoisky. He was followed to the grave by a large number of the most respectable citizens of Grand Rapids, and by nearly all the Indians of his tribe.

Notwithstanding the treaty already mentioned, the Indians never moved to the proposed reservation west of the Mississippi, but were, after considerable persuasion, induced to move to a reservation within this State, where they still reside, though reduced in numbers.

CHAPTER X.

EARLY SETTLEMENT OF ADA—RIX ROBINSON—HIS LIFE AMONG THE INDIANS—HIS ATTACHMENT TO THEM—SCENE OF A TOWN MEETING—THE VILLAGE OF ADA.

WE WILL now leave Grand Rapids and observe the events that were transpiring in other parts of Kent county during that period through which the reader ha been conducted in the preceding chapters.

The township of Ada originally embraced a large tract of country, including several of what are now the adjacent towns. It was of Ada as it then existed that Rix Robinson was elected the first Supervisor. The first entry upon the records is under date of 1835, to the effect that Norman Smith was elected Supervisor by one majority, he receiving in all thirty-two votes. The whole number of votes cast was only sixty-one. The sight of a town meeting in those days was an interesting one. Here they come, one by one, from the different points of the compass, hard-working, honest men. It is a gala day with them. They meet, perhaps, for the first time in months. They go early in the morning and stay late at night. They urge their brief political campaign in their homely way. They enjoy as well as perform their duty, and then part for the scenes of stern labor.

One of the most prominent of the early settlers was Rix Robinson, the first white man who settled in the township. For a long time he was engaged in the fur trade with the Indians on the Grand River. Alone, he traversed the forests in the interests of the American Fur Company, surrounded with savages by nature, and sometimes by deed, but was unmolested by them. The spirit of the natives had already been somewhat subdued by the influence of christianity, and devoted missionaries were then laboring among them. A tribe of these Indians remained near the town of Ada until 1860, when they sold their lands and removed to Pentwater. During the latter years of their residence on these lands, they cultivated the soil, and built respectable residences, had well organized schools and comfortable churches. They were of the Roman Catholic faith.

Mr. Robinson, during his sojourn and life among the Indians, became remarkably attached to them; so much so that he chose one of their daughters as his partner for life, with whom he still lives. They have but one son, and he is well known throughout Grand River Valley as an energetic business man, and more recently as a local preacher of the gospel.

Mr. Robinson's life is fraught with toil and peril, and actual suffering. "It is pleasant," said an old resident, "to sit and listen while 'Uncle Rix' tells of the dark days in the history of his experience. I have often heard him repeat the story of the nights he spent in the woods alone, far from any house; of fording streams in winter; of encounters with wolves and other animals; of the poor log house with its chimney; of sickness and death in the family, with no attending physician, and so on through the long list. But I was not the only delighted one. What a change came over the countenance of the aged man as he recounted those scenes!"

The experience of the pioneers of Ada was similar to that of other townships; they worked hard, endured

---

much, and enjoyed much.   They. lived a noble life, although it was a life, perhaps, few of us would choose. Among the other early settlers in Ada, I will mention Edward Robinson, who settled in 1830; Torrey Smith, A. H. Riggs and Edward Pettis, in 1836; Peter McLean, R. G. Chaffee, Hezekiah Howell, E. McCormick, P. Fingleton, Gurden Chapel, John Findlay and J. S. Schenck in 1840 to 1845.

The principal rivers in the township are the Grand and Thornapple. Grand River crosses the township from the northwest to the southwest, and is navigable for small crafts. Before the completion of the Detroit and Milwaukee Railroad steamboats passed up the river as far as Ionia.   Chase's Lake is the only one worthy of mention.   It is located on sections two and eleven, and contains about one hundred and sixty acres.   The timber is mostly oak, the land being what is usually termed "oak openings." The soil is rather sandy, being well adapted to fruit culture. It is well suited, also, to the production of the different kinds of grain.

Ada village was laid out into lots when the Detroit and

Milwaukee Railroad was built—about the year 1858—
and although one or more additional plats have been
made, its growth seems to be quite slow. It is located
on sections thirty-three and thirty-four, near the conflu
ence of the Thornapple in Grand River, ten miles, by
railroad, from Grand Rapids. It possesses a very good
water power, which is only now beginning to be improved. There are already several extensive mills on
the Thornapple River, most of which are doing a profitable business.

The school houses and educational facilities of the
village are as good as any place of equal population in
the State. The business interests of the place are growing rapidly, and will, no doubt, continue to increase.

CHAPTER XI.

ALPINE—ITS EARLY SETTLEMENT—INCIDENTS OF PIO-
NEER LIFE—THE FIRST SETTLERS—TOWN MEETINGS
—THE MILLS—SOIL, ETC.

ALPINE is one of the west tier of townships, and is
bounded on the north by Sparta, on the east by Plain-

---

field, on the south by Walker, and on the west by the township of Wright, Ottawa county. The first settlers were Solomon Wright and family, who came from Wayne county, N. Y., in the year 1837, and located on the south line, near Indian Creek. The family consisted of the old gentleman and lady and five sons, Benjamin, Solomon, Noodiah, Andrew and Jeremiah, only one of whom remains in the township, and that is Solomon. The old people are both dead, one son lost his life in the late war, one is living at Lowell, and two are in Walker.

In the year 1840 John Coffee and Richmond Gooding came from Ohio, penetrated the forests nearly five miles beyond Wright, and settled near the west line of the township. For many years this was considered " the jumping-off place," as they termed it, there being no settlements north of them, and, in fact, no house in any direction nearer than three or four miles. About the same time Jacob Snyder, a German, settled on section thirty-five, and another German, named John Plattee, on section thirty-six, in the southeast* corner of the township. A short time previous, Turner Hills and family came from Vermont and located in the east part of the township on section thirteen, where, for several years, they were the northernmost settlers. Mr. Hills died several years ago, but the widow and two sons survived him in active and profitable industry.

Among other pioneers who settled in various parts of the township at an early day, I will mention Noel Hopkins, Baltas Schaffer, Peter Schlick, James Snowden, Sherman Pearsall, John B. Colton, A. B. Tones, Thompsom Kasson, Joseph Hipler, John Ellis, Edward Wheeler,

Hervey Wilder, Joseph Bullen, Moses Ramsdell, John J. Downer, Hiram Stevenson, Artemus Hilton, Henry S. Church, Charles Anderson, Francis Greenley and the Boyds, Denisons, Meads, Bremers, Davenports and Cordes.

Many and varied were the privations endured by these early settlers. We, who have never been pioneers, cannot fully appreciate the sufferings, the trials and hardships which were their lot. Contemplate a journey to Grand Rapids with an ox team, over rough roads, with a grist for the mill; of a return in the night with its many perplexities, now and then losing the indistinct road, with a consequent delay of half an hour; of finding trees blown across the way, preventing further progress until they have been removed by the use of the axe, and so on through the list.

Again imagine, if you can, the loneliness of a family coming from a thickly settled part of the country, and making a home in the wilderness, with no actual neighbors; with no schools; with no churches; and, in fact, with no associations except those of their own fireside.

Little time can be spared for social intercourse, even at home. The round of duties consumes each day but the Sabbath, which is, indeed, to them a day of holy rest.

I do not wish to be understood as stating that there are no enjoyments connected with such a life. Situated as the pioneer of this place was, in an unbroken forest, with every stroke of the axe, and with every effort made toward improvement, he seemed to be hewing out a little world of his own. Every acre added to the cleared space added more than its proportional amount of pleasure to the soul of the laborer. He looked forward to the time when his broad acres should be seen clothed with the rich yellow grain of a plenteous harvest, and he looked not in vain.

Alpine was united with the township of Walker in 1847. Its first independent township meeting was held at the school house in the southeast corner of the township on the 5th day of April, 1847, which resulted in the election of the following named persons as officers: Supervisor, Edward Wheeler; Clerk, C. D. Shenich; Treasurer, Casper Cordes; Justices, Wm. H. Withey,

---

John Coffee, John Colton and John Tuxbury. The next annual meeting was held at the house of Edward Wheeler, near the centre of the township. Soon after a small log school house was erected on the corner of Mr. Wheeler's farm, one-half mile east of the centre, and was used as a place of holding township meetings until about the year 1860, when a fine Town Hall building was erected on the northeast corner of section twenty-one.

Alpine, which is said to have derived its name from the supposition of many of the early settlers that it was chiefly timbered with pine, is not what its name indicates. There was originally considerable pine along the larger streams. At one time several saw mills were located on Mill Creek, and were doing a brisk business, but now there is hardly enough pine left to sustain two.

The soil of the beech and maple timbered portions of Alpine, which comprise about two-thirds of the township, is generally clay or loam. Indeed, this is a township of good land, well adapted to the productions of

---

both grain and fruit. The good looking orchards and the loads of apples, peaches, plums, pears, etc., as well as the excellent yields of wheat and other grain, speak for themselves. The soil of the pine timbered portions is sandy, but it grows fair crops when well cultivated and improved.

CHAPTER XII.

EARLY HISTORY OF BOWNE—THE FIRST SETTLERS—A WOMAN'S COURAGE—INTERESTING INCIDENTS OF PIONEER LIFE—WOLVES, BEARS AND INDIANS.

IN 1837 Mr. Jonathan Thomas, of Ovid, New York, came and settled in the northwestern portion of Bowne, bringing with him his family and a friend named Frederick Thompson. Mr. Israel Graves and family, and Mr. Wm. Wooley and family came about the same time. They came by water to Toledo, and thence to this township with ox teams, making the trip from Toledo in about two weeks. They proceeded to build houses and clear up farms. The first house they built, and the first within the town, is still standing and is preserved as a relic of the past, and as a contrast with the present. It is built of logs, about twelve by fourteen feet square, without any chambers and with only one door and one window and a "Shake" roof. Near this Mr. Thomas built two other houses and a small log building for an office for himself.

Mr. Thomas was taken sick soon after his arrival, and continued so until the next winter, when he was visited by his son-in-law, Mr. John Harris, who determined to remove him to his home in New York. He fixed a bed in a sleigh and started in December, 1837. They made the whole distance with a sleigh, dragging through Northern Ohio in the slush and mud, and occupying over four weeks in making the journey.

During the summer of 1837, when they got out of provisions, Mr. Thomas, although quite ill at the time, had his bed fixed in a wagon, and, taking his whip, started his ox team for Kalamazoo. He found it necessary to go a few miles beyond there and buy wheat, bring it back to Kalamazoo and have it ground.

When these families first moved into the township there were a great many Indians there. They found them good neighbors when they were sober, but when they could get liquor they were quarrelsome, and occasioned considerable trouble. One came to Mr. Thompson's house one day when there was no one in but his wife. He sat down in a rocking chair before the fire and rocked himself over into the fire-place. Mrs. Thompson pulled him out of the fire, and he became enraged and attempted to stab her; but when she picked up an axe and threatened to take his life if he did not leave, he made a quick retreat.

At another time a lot of Indians came up on their ponies, when the men were gone, and ordered Mrs. Wooley to get them something to eat. She ran to her door and called for Mrs. Thompson, who came to her relief, affecting to be brave and fearless; but the old chief ordered her to go back to her wigwam and get him something to eat. The poor woman obeyed, trembling with fear, and got the best dinner she could under the circumstances, setting her table with her nicest spread and best dishes she had. The chief ate his meal alone at her house and declared himself much pleased. He told her that she was a "brave squaw," and that they would not harm any of them then; but after a certain number of moons they were going to kill all the whites in the country.

A number of the families I have mentioned soon became discouraged and went back, while those who remained were seven miles from any white neighbors.

At one time when Mr. Thompson went to Kalamazoo to mill, owing to his oxen straying away while at the mill, he was detained from his home eight days. His

---

wife remained at the house alone until noon of the eighth day, when her suspense became so great that she could not bear it any longer, and she started on foot for the nearest neighbor's, seven miles distant. After completing half the journey, she was met by a white man. She enquired after her husband, was told of the circumstances which caused his delay, and that he was on the road and would be home before night. He advised her to return home, but her reply was, "I will never stop until I see my husband."

These were dark and romantic days in the history of Bowne. Packs of wolves were often seen prowling in the outskirts of the woods, and bears frequently came within a few yards of the houses. For several years they used to go to "Scale's Prairie" to meeting, but after a time the population increased and the little town could boast its own Minister.

In the spring of 1838 quite a large number of settlers came in, and soon the desolating forests began to disappear. Civilization had procured a strong foothold, and prosperity followed in abundance. Excellent schools soon followed the churches, and the increase of population, industry and wealth have ever since marked the progress of the place.

The first township election was held in 1838, resulting in the election of the following staff of officers: Supervisor, Abner D. Thomas; Clerk, Abel Ford; Treasurer, James M. Nash; Justices, Steven Johnston, Benjamin J. Lee, Levi Stone, Henry D. Francisco; Commissioners of Highways, Loren B. Tyler, Henry D. Francisco, W. H. Stone; Constable, Oliver A. Stone.

CHAPTER XIII.

BYRON—PIONEER LIFE—"RAISING" THE FIRST LOG HOUSE—ROAST POTATOES THE ONLY FOOD—FIGHTING THE WOLVES—THE FIRST TOWN MEETING.

IN THE summer of 1836 Byron was an unbroken wilderness. The ruthless arm of the white man, armed with that terribly destructive weapon, the axe, had never been lifted midst the beautiful forests that crowned the sloping hills and shaded the broad green vales. The trackless forests stood in the beauty in which the God of Nature created it. But the day for the pioneer's axe had come, and very soon it was heard in its depths.

During the summer of this year Mr. Nathan Boynton located a farm on section five, and selected a place to build a house, on a little hill near the forks of Rush Creek. Mr. Boynton returned to Grandville, where he was taken sick, but, in August or September, sent his brothers, William and Jerry, to build a house for him. The only guide they had was the section line. This they followed until they came to the line between the present townships of Byron and Wyoming, where they, not knowing that there was a variation in the section lines of the different ranges of townships, lost the line, and were a considerable time finding the place Nathan had selected for his residence. After finding it they proceeded to erect a house. It was built of small logs, such as they could carry and put up. The roof was of small basswood, split in two parts, and gutters cut with an axe on the flat side. One tier of these was laid with the flat side up and the other with the flat side down, so that the outside edge of the upper tier fitted into the gutter of the lower. The floor and door of the house were made of plank, or, as woodsmen usually call them, "puncheons," split from basswood trees. The fire place was built of clay, which Mr. Boynton mixed by treading with his bare feet, and was built up with small twigs. The chimney was built of split sticks, laid up in the same kind of mortar. This fire-place and chimney were used for several years and did good service. Such was the first house erected in the township of Byron.

Jerry and William Boynton soon after located farms on sections eight and nine, respectively, and commenced improving them, which, by their skill and energy, they have rendered very productive, In 1837 Mr. John Harmon located on section nine, and during the same year Mr. H. Kellogg located on section three and Mr. James B. Jewell on section nine. Mr. Ella Judson followed in 1838. The latter gentleman says that when he built his log house, he had to go a distance of four miles to get men to help " raise," and could get only eight men at that.

The settlers that followed were Mr. Larkin Ball, Peter Goldin, Eli Crossett, Amelek Taylor, Alden Coburn, Benj. Robihson, William Olmstead, Samuel Hubbel, and Henry A. Vannest. When Mr. Hubbel's house was " raised," the job could not be completed in one day, and it was so far for the hands to go home, that they stayed and camped out one night, and finished "raising" the next day. All the hard working men had for supper and breakfast was roast potatoes.

Among the settlers who came to this township in 1843–4 were Mr. Fox, Mr. Ezekiel Cook, Mr. Tuft, E. R. Ide and James K. McKenney.

When Mr. Cook moved into the woods they had no neighbors nearer than four miles, and their nearest post-office was at Grand Rapids, a distance of fourteen miles, through an unbroken wilderness. When Mr. Kennedy moved on his place there was no road from there to Grandville except as he followed the trails that wound around through the woods. When Mr. McKenney moved into his house there were neither windows, doors or floor in the house. The next day after moving in Mr. McKenney was taken sick and was confined to his bed for two weeks, and before he was able to build a fireplace and chimney, there was two feet of snow. During all this time Mrs. McKenney had to do all her cooking out of doors by a log fire. Those were hard days. There was hardly a ray of happiness let into this desolate household. The storm and wind beat through the open windows, and sang mournfully through their forest home.

When Mr. Tuft moved on to his place the only signs of a house he had was a small sled-load of lumber. He began to build in December, and his family shivered around until the rude hut was completed.

During the year 1845 Messrs. Corkins, Barney, Clark S. Wilson and Willian Davidson settled within the limits of the township. Among other early settlers I will mention Josiah R. Holden, Bradly Weaver, David Prindle, Carlos Weaver and Prentice Weaver, Eli Young, and James M. Barney. The latter gentleman came during the famous "wolf year." Mr. Young says he killed one of these ferocious animals within one rod of his own door with his dog and corn-cutter.

Mr. William Boynton would often, before this period, when he was obliged to work at Grandville to get provisions for the support of his family, work all day, get the proceeds of his labor in provisions, and at dark start for home, a distance of about five miles through the woods, while the wolves were howling on every side, and sometimes coming within reach of the good, stout cudgel which he carried.

The first year Mr. James Barney lived in his house he had to keep his cow and calf in a high log pen near by at nights to save them from the wolves. He says that one night, after being kept awake until near morning, he took his gun just at daylight and sallied forth, determined on vengeance. When he went out the wolves retreated for a short distance, but when he came into a thicket of bushes they surrounded him; he backed up against a tree and they kept him there for about two hours. He shot at them several times, but the bushes were so thick he did not kill any, although they would come so near that he could hear their teeth snapping together. After this year the wolves became, happily, scarce.

The first township meeting was held at the house of

Mr. Charles H. Oakes, in Grandville, on Monday, the second day of May, 1836. The following list of officers were there chosen: Supervisor, Sideon H. Gordon; Clerk, Isaac A. Allen; Assessors, Eli Yeomans, Ephraim P. Walker and Justin Brooks; Justices, G. H. Gordon, Robert Howlett and E. P. Walker; Collector, L. French; Commissioners of Highways, G. H. Gordon, Eli Yoomans and H. Pitts; School Commissioners, Joseph B. Copeland, Sanford Buskirk and James Lockwood; School Inspectors, G. H. Gordon, Isaac A. Allen and Eli Yeomans; Overseers of the Poor, E P. Walker and Justin Brooks; Constables, L. French and Sanford Buskirk.

During the first year the settlement of Byron progressed very slowly. It required a brave heart and a strong arm to encounter the dangers and hardships consequent upon opening up a new and heavily timbered country. But gradually the forests yielded to the pioneer's axe, and beautiful fields and thrifty orchards, comfortable dwellings and well filled barns have taken its place. Byron has already become one of the foremost agricultural townships in Kent county.

With varied soil, adapted to nearly all the different branches of husbandry, and especially to fruit growing, and the very best facilities for marketing its produce, its farmers must soon stand among the best and most wealthy in the State.

Byron is traversed by two railroads, the northern branch of the Lake Shore and Michigan Southern Railroad, and the Grand Rapids and Indiana Railroad. The Lake Shore and Michigan Southern runs north and south through the town, and has two stations on its line in Byron, called Byron Center and North Byron. The Grand Rapids and Indiana runs north and south through the eastern part of the township, and has one station near the south part of the town.

This township is composed of what is known as "timbered lands," comprising within its limits nearly every variety of trees known in this climate. It is quite well watered by Birch and Rush Creeks, and the springs and numerous small streams that form these creeks.

Almost all signs of pioneer life have passed away, and the greater part of the township is being rapidly im

---

proved. The old pioneer farmers are nearly all wealthy, and take pleasure in telling the stories of earlier and darker days.

CHAPTER XIV.

CALEDONIA—ITS RESOURCES AND ADVANTAGES—SOME INTERESTING INCIDENTS OF EARLY TRAVEL—THE PIONEER TAVERNS—KENT'S TAVERN—INCIDENTS OF EARLY SETTLEMENT.

CALEDONIA is one of the southern tier of townships of Kent county. It is traversed from south to north by the Thornapple river, which divides it into two nearly equal parts. The banks of the river are high, and the country on both sides of the river is high and rolling. On the east side of the river you have the " openings,' the soil being sandy and gravelly, with a slight mixture of clay, and is timbered principally with oak and hickory. The soil on this side of the river is especially adapted to wheat and fruit, but produces good crops of all kinds of grain and most grasses.

There are several lakes on this side of the river. The

shore on the southeast side is sandy, and on the north-west mucky and marshy. The Coldwar, or Little Thornapple enters Caledonia on section thirty-six, and empties into the Thornapple on section twenty-five. The west side of the river is all "timbered lands," producing all of the kinds of timber that usually grow in this climate on such lands. All kinds of fruit grow almost to perfection on this soil. There are a great many fine farms in this township, and its agricultural resources are being developed very fast.

Nestled among the hills on the banks of the Thornapple, in the northern part of the township, is the thriving little village of Alaska, formerly known as North Brownville. It has a very pleasant location, and is an active, enterprising place.

Mr. Asahel Kent was the first settler in the township, settling on section thirty-five in 1838. Mr. Kent, and after his death Mrs. Kent, kept a public house, which became quite famous in the pioneer settlement. It was called "Kent's Tavern," and the route leading to it from the outside world was call "Gull Trail." Mrs. Kent afterwards married Mr. Peter McNaughton, and the place became equally well known to travelers on the Battle Creek and Grand Rapids stage route as "McNaughton's."

I will give a few reminiscenses of this stage route here, in order to contrast the present mode of travel with that patronized in Caledonia in 1839. One person says that in this year, he then a boy of only fourteen, made the journey with three or four others from Grand Rapids to Detroit, and that they stopped at "Kent's" over night, and he, with others of the travelers, had to sleep out in a sort of shed, as the house was so small it would not accommodate them.

At this time this was the only house from Ada to "Leonard's," a distance of seventeen miles. About two years after this gentleman commenced to drive stage on this route, and drove for several years. The road at this time wound round through the woods, and it was no uncommon thing to get "stuck" in the mud, or to overset. At one time, a very dark stormy night, they broke an axeltree about six miles south of Ada, and the passengers, five or six in number, had to walk through mud and snow to that place, as it was the nearest settlement.

At another time, Hon. John Ball, Mrs. Thomas B. Church and others were in the stage; they overset in a mud hole and the passengers were all precipitated into the water. It was very dark, and Mr. Fred Church, then an infant, was nearly suffocated before they found him. At another time Hon. Wm. A. Richmond and Hon. Harvey P. Yale were his only passengers; the roads were muddy and badly rutted out and the night fearfully dark.   Mr. Yale fell asleep, and the wheels striking into a deep rut pitched him out into the mud. After a hearty laugh he resumed his place and the stage moved along.

But let us go back to the early settlement of Caledonia.   Among the first comers were James Minsey, Eber Moffitt, Hiram McNeil, Peter McNaughton, Levi Tobey, John Sinclair, O. B. Barber, John Pattison, Henry Jackson, Wm. H. Brown and Warren S. Hale.   Mr. Lyman Hale was the first settler on the west side of the river. Mr. William H. Brown erected the first saw mill at Alaska.

Among the incidents connected with the early settlement of the township, showing some of the hardships the pioneers had to endure, I will give the following: Mr. Wm. H. Brown, previous to his settlement at Brownsville, but after he had located his land, lived at "Scale's Prairie," or Middleville.   Having occasion to go there one winter, he started from home in the morning on horse back, intending to return the same day.   After making his observations and examining his land, about

---

where the village of Alaska now stands, he started for home; night soon came on, and after endeavoring to follow his track for a while, he found out that he was lost. He dismounted, and as he had nothing to kindle a fire with, cleared the snow out of the path with his feet and covered it with some bark from a dry tree, and walked to and fro over it all night. When morning came he mounted his horse, and, after riding for some time, came out at the Green Lake House. His friends had started after him in the morning, expecting to find him frozen to death, and followed his tracks until they found him at Green Lake.

But in Caledonia, as in all other settlements in Michigan, pioneering has mostly passed into history. It is now a flourishing township, the inhabitants rejoicing in the ample rewards of labor.

CHAPTER XV.

Cannon and Cascade—Early Settlement of these Places—Incidents of the Pioneers—The First Farms—Names of the Early Settlers.

Cannon, originally a part of Plainfield, lies northwest of Grand Rapids, having Courtland on the north, Grattan on the east, Ada on the south, and Plainfield on the west. In the year 1837 the first farm was entered within its territory by Andrew Watson, who came with his family, accompanied by A. D. W. Stout and family, and settled on section thirty, where Mr. Watson and his aged wife resided for many years after. In the following year came Isaac Tomlinson, locating upon section twenty-seven, in a beautiful situation commanding an extensive and enchanting view of the Grand River and its beautiful valley.   In 1839 Wm. M. Miller settled upon section nineteen.

The date of emigration had now fairly set in, and the waving forests rolled back before a hundred pioneer axes.   Among the new-comers in 1840 were James Thomas, Oliver Lovejoy, Mr. Rood and Rev. Mr. Frieze.

Among those who distinguished themselves in developing the town, I will mention M. A. Patrick and E. B. Smith.   In 1845 the separation from Plainfield was effected, and the township was created into a separate town, under the name, by mistake of the Legislature, of Churchtown, assuming its present name, however, in honor of its principal village at its first town meeting, held to complete its organization, on the first Monday of April, 1846, at the house of C. Slaght, in Cannonsburg.

Cannon presents a great variety of surface, soil and productions.   Its main staples raised for the market are wheat, wool, corn and apples.   Of the former, large quantities are exported, and its rolling lands and dry, healthful climate make its wool-growing a success.   Lying within the great Western fruit belt, and being blessed with a deep, pliable soil, it is eminently adapted to horticultural pursuits.   Of this its people are fully aware, and we find in many flourishing orchards, apples, pears, peaches, cherries and currants abound, while grapes and the small fruits are fast becoming specialties.

While its business centers have not reached to any great importance, its rural districts are marked with thrift and enterprise.   Comfort smiles from its tasteful dwellings nestled amid shade and bloom, while an abounding plenty is stored in its spacious barns.   This township is remarkable for the industry and the wealth of its inhabitants.

Cannonsburg, the only business center of any note within the town, was founded in 1842, an Indian war trail its only thoroughfare, and the settler's axe the only key that would open the forest gates that guarded its entrance. In 1844 and 1845 its mills were erected by E. B. Bostwick and H. T. Judson, and a store opened. As an inducement to permanent settlement the village was platted in 1845, and Mr. Bostwick, the enterprising business agent of LeGrand Cannon, its proprietor, (an eastern capitalist and large land-holder in the town), was instructed to give a village lot to each resident not otherwise provided for; thus twenty-five lots were given away.

The town received the name it now bears in honor of its founder, who testified his appreciation of the distinction conferred by presenting the village with a small ordinance, bearing his name and date. This is treasured by the authorities as a memento of early times, and used

---

on the 4th of July and other holiday occasions, wakening the echoes of memory in many a heart as its thunders reverberate among the hills that completely surround the little village.

Cannonsburg is situated on both sides of Bear Creek, and is a flourishing and well-to-do settlement.

Cascade lies lies in the second tier of townships from the south and east line of the county, and is bounded on the north by Ada, on the east by Lowell, on the south by Caledonia, and on the west by Paris. At first it was a part of the township of Ada. Louis Cook, a native of New Jersey, is said to have been the first settler within the township of Cascade. He came in 1836, and was soon followed by Hiram Laraway, Ed. Linen, James May, David Petted, John Farrell, James and William Annis, Michael Matthews, Patrick, Christopher and Michael Eardley.

In 1838, Frederick A. Marsh, of New York, united in marriage with Olive Guild, a daughter of Joel Guild, one of the pioneer settlers of Grand Rapids, and began domestic life in the unbroken wilderness, one mile north and west of where Cascade village now stands. Mr. Marsh lived to see the forest yield its place to cultivated fields and comfortable dwellings, and to have a school house erected on his own land. He was killed by a fall from his wagon, in 1856. In the winter of 1841, Mr. Laraway was frozen to death while making the journey between Ada and his own lonely residence. His widow braved the hardships of pioneer life and trained up three sons and a daughter to lives of usefulness.

Peter and George Teeple came to Cascade during those years, joining the settlers on the west side of the Thorn-apple, while the eastern side was yet unmarked by civilization, but inhabited by about three hundred and fifty Ottawa Indians.

In 1841, Peter Whitney, of Ohio, moved his family into that part of Cascade known as Whitneyville, and E. D. Gore, of Massachusetts, selected a site for his future home near the center of the township, in the summer of 1842. Next came Horace Sears, from New York, and Zerah and Ezra Whitney, and settled in Whitneyville.

In the spring of 1845, Asa W. Denison and family, from Massachusetts, and George H. Denison came and joined the settlers on the west side of the Thornapple. Coming in on the State Road from Battle Creek to Grand Rapids, the teams, women and children of the company were obliged to wait at Ezra Whitney's public house for the road to be "chopped out," between that point and the river, theirs being the first teams that passed over the road. At Cascade they forded the Thornapple with their household goods, and found timber on the ground for the erection of the old Ferry House (now Cascade Hotel), which was at that time owned by D. S. T. Weller. During that year the house was so far completed as to admit of occupancy, and the first ferry boat commenced its trips just above where the bridge now spans the stream. D. S. T. Weller then owned the plat of land now occupied by Cascade village, although first purchased by Joel Guild; and it was at that time staked out into lots of one acre each. This was done as the fine fal on the river gave hopes for the speedy erection of mills at that place, some of the most sanguine settlers proph-

---

esying that Cascade would outstrip Grand Rapids in the strife for precedence.

During the year 1845, a disease, which our old settlers denominate the "black tongue," broke out among the Indians near Whitneyville, reducing their number to two hundred in about two weeks. The band now became wasted by disease and removal, until less than fifty remained at the time of their removal to the Indian reservation, in 1856.

In 1846 another family was added to the few settlers on the east side of the river—Jared Strong, the first settler in the forest between this place and the town of Ada. The following year a school was opened in a little log house on the river bank for the children in that vicinity.

The first township meeting was held at Whitneyville, April 3d, 1848, and the following township officers were elected:

Supervisor, Peter Teeple; Clerk, John R. Stewart; Treasurer, Asa W. Denison; School Inspectors, James H. Woodworth, Thomas I. Seeley; Commissioners of

Highways, Ezra Whitney, Fred A. Marsh, William De-golia; Justices of the Peace, Leonard Stewart, Zerah Whitney; Assessors, Thosmas I. Seeley, Harry Clark; Constables, Morris Denison, D. P. Corson, Wm. Cook, Peter J. Whitney.

From this day Cascade marched forward to success with even progress. Commerce followed the pioneer's axe and stores were soon opened, and it is, to-day, one of the most thrifty places of its size in the State. The town can boast several school buildings of decidedly fine appearance. It has several churches, and enjoys all the blessings of wealth and prosperity.

CHAPTER XVI.

Township of Gaines—Incidents of Early Settle-ment—Interesting Incidents—Capturing the "Gull Prairie Wolf"—The Red School House —First Town Meeting.

Gaines is situated in the southern tier of townships of Kent county. The first settler in this township was Alexander Clark, who located on section eight in the

---

spring of 1837. He was joined in the following autumn by Alex. L. Bonck. Gaines at this period had little to recommend her to the eyes of civilization, being nothing more or less than thirty-six square miles of wilderness. Yet, to the hardy, enterprising pioneers her heavy forests of beech and maple, and, in some localities, pine and oak, an abundant supply of fresh water, with an average share of bears, wolves, deer and wild turkeys, possessed a charm that captivated the enterprising settlers.

At this time the only thoroughfare within the limits of the territory of Gaines was a road known as the "Old Gull Road," running a zig-zag course from north to south. The line of settlement followed the course of this road, and to-day we find some of the richest farms on this line. It was afterwards straightened as the township became settled to correspond with the section lines, and became a stage route from Grand Rapids to Kalamazoo until the completion of the plank road in 1854.

Gaines, aside from her agricultural prospects, offered

but little inducement to business men. Plaster and Buck creeks both rise near the centre of the township, but are too small during most of the year for profitable mill sites. There was, however, a small water mill erected on the latter stream about the year 1852, by Esech Burlingame, which is still running, and which cut the lumber for some of the first frame buildings in the township.

Most of the settlers of Gaines, as is usual, were poor, having barely means enough to enable them to purchase their lands of the Government for $1.25 an acre, get their families and household goods transported through the wilderness, and gain a foothold on their farms. But with persistent energy they set to work and the heavy forests began to disappear. It was soon found to be one of the richest tracts in the vicinity for agricultural purposes, and at the present date is one of the best in the country.

The first attempt at organization was as a part of Paris in 1839, but in the year 1848 it was organized under the name of Gaines, and the first township meeting was held at the old red school house. The following law was passed at the first meeting : "On motion of Orson Cook, it was voted that a tax of two dollars and fifty cents be raised for every wolf killed in the township."

Wolves were rather troublesome neighbors in those days, and the author of the motion probably owed them a grudge for their former depredations. Wolves made frequent visits to the early settlers, and would make the very earth tremble with their howlings and complaints to the intruders of their time-honored homes.

One occupation of the boys and larger girls of that day used to be to fire the old stumps about the place in the evening to scare away the wolves. About the year 1846 there was a wolf who had her beat from this vicinity to Gull Prairie, in Barry County, and was known as the "Gull Prairie Wolf," who usually made the round trip once a week. The dogs would not molest her, and she seemed to care for neither man nor beast. She had been caught once in a steel trap, and all efforts to entrap her again were for a long time unsuccessful. Even the children, in time, seemed to distinguish her voice from other wolves, and were in the habit of listening for her on certain nights. She seldom disappointed them, and made night hideous with her howls. She finally killed four sheep in one night on the premises of Mr. Mesnard. Mr. Jones, who lived near, requested the owner to leave one of the carcasses, which the wolf had partially devoured, and he did so. Messrs. Jones and Cook then held a council of war, at which they concluded to make one more effort to entrap her. Accordingly, two traps were set near the carcass. But on her next visit she contrived to remove the carcass several rods, taking care to avoid the traps. Another consultation resulted in more traps, Four were set, placing in the intermediate spaces small pieces of iron, which were left in sight, while the traps were carefully concealed. This time they outwitted her and she was caught in one of the traps. Early on the following morning Messrs. Jones and Cook took the trail in pursuit. They overtook her near Duncan Lake, caught her and attempted to bring her home alive, but the wolf acted so badly that they were compelled to abandon the project. They brought home the pelt for which they received one dollar, and ten and a half dollars in county and State bounties.

But the wolves and their allies, the bears and wild-cats, have disappeared, and the township has become largely settled and improved. At the first township meeting only thirty-five votes were polled, but to-day her population is nearly two thousand. Thrifty farms greet you at every turn; comfortable frame cottages take the place of the log huts of the pioneer; good roads

---

on section lines traverse all parts of the township ; and from thirty-six square miles of wilderness she has grown in thirty-six years to an enterprising, thrifty agricultural town.

The first school was taught in a log house, erected by Mr. Clark about the year 1842.   This, in a short time, was removed to give place to a frame building painted red, and known throughout the county as the red school house, which was succeeded, in 1863, by the present elegant structure on the same sight.   There are ten school houses in the township, all comfortable frame buildings.

The society of United Brethren built a church on section twenty-eight in 1867, which, although plain and modest, is neat and tasty—an honor to the association and an ornament to the community.   It is situated on one of the most elevated points of the township, and can be seen for miles around.

The Grand River Valley Railroad runs through the territory of Gaines, and is now being a valuable aid to its progress.

The first township officers were : Peter Van Lee, Supervisor ; James M. Pelton, Clerk ; Charles Kelley, Treasurer ; Joseph Blain, Josiah Drake and Robert R. Jones, Justices of the Peace ; Foster Kelley and Abram T. Andrews, Assessors ; Daniel Rice, Levi M. Dewey and William Kelley, Commissioners of Highways ; R. Mesnard and A. T. Andrews, School Inspectors ; O. Cook and Levi Cheney,·Poor Directors ; L. W. Sanford, J. E. Guild, T. Kelley and Daniel Williams, Constables.

CHAPTER XVII.

Grattan and Lowell—Incidents of Early Settlement—The First Marriage in Grattan—Early Settlers on the Flat River—The First Log Huts.

Grattan is one of the eastern tier of townships. It was originally a part of Vergennes, and was created into a separate town in 1846. It was largely settled in its southern portion by emigrants directly from Ireland.

In 1843 the first settlement was made within the limits of the town, by Dennis and John McCarthy and Richard Giles. In 1844, Luther B. Cook built the first house north of Seeley's Creek. Among the early settlers who followed were C. Close, J. Watkins, Henry Green, Anthony King, V. W. Caukin, M. Kennedy, and W. McCarthy.

Prominent among the settlers who came in 1845 were John P. Weeks, Orson Nichoson, William Byrnes, and A. Green. Of these old settlers most reside where they first located.

There are many interesting personal experiences incident to the early settlement of this town. Out of many of these I will mention one. A widely known and highly respectable couple, still residents of the town, wished to get married, but there was no functionary in that part of Kent county vested with authority to perform the ceremony. A well-known Justice of Ionia county chanced to be visiting at the house where the parties were, and their dilemma was made known to him. Of course he had no jurisdiction in Kent, but the county line was only half a mile away, and a walk through the forest was proposed and agreed to. The Justice took his stand in Ionia county, and the bride and bridegroom, protesting, would not leave the county to be married, joined hands just over the line, and in the presence of a few friends, gathered beneath the grand old oaks, on the pleasant afternoon of July 28th, 1844, the twain were made one, to their own gratification as well as that of the spectators.

In those early days the settler, with his axe, cut the way for his future home, and in the absence of stores; grist and saw-mills, supplied, by his own ingenuity, the actual necessities of himself and family. To-day, all the conveniences of civilized life are at hand, and well cultivated farms, and the more than ordinary wealth displayed in dwellings are highly significant of the great enterprise and consequent prosperity of the people.

Grattan has not only maintained an honorable position in the county, but has also made its record among the dignitaries of the State. Among those who have represented that section in the State Legislature are Hon. Volney W. Caukin and Hon. M. C. Watkins.

Lowell lies north of Bowne and south of Vergennes. It is one of the eastern tier of townships in Kent county. Its soil, timber and productions are greatly diversified.

The soil of the southern portion is mostly clay or loam, lies very high, and is generally level and well adapted to farming purposes. The north half is considerably broken by the Grand and Flat rivers, and Lakes McEwing, Pratt, Morse, Stoughton, and several swamps. This township is well supplied with stone for building purposes, and in some parts they are used to some extent for fencing, especially in the northwest corner of the township.

In the year 1829, Daniel Marsac came from Detroit and went among the Indians in the vicinity of the present village of Lowell as a trader, although a regular trading post was not established there until 1831, when Mr. Marsac built a log hut on the south side of the Grand River, near the present site of J. Koff & Co's extensive chair works.

When Mr. Marsac first pitched his tent within the borders of Kent county, then an almost unbroken wilderness, the only roads were the Indian trails, and the only means of navigation was the canoe, or the "dug-out," as it is sometimes called; or for more extensive transportation a raft made of poles or small logs fastened together.

In the spring of 1835, a family by the name of Robinson, numbering in all forty-four persons, set out from the State of New York, and, arriving at Detroit, embarked on a small vessel for Grand Haven, *via* Mackinaw.   On the 7th day of June of that year they reached the mouth of Grand River, and, putting their household goods on rafts, poled their way up the river and settled in Ottawa and Kent counties.   These were only a part of the Robinsons; Rix Robinson had been trading with the Indians at Ada for several years previous.   A year later another brother, named Lewis, came with his family and settled on the west bank of Flat River, in the south part of what is now the village of Lowell.   He was soon followed by Rodney, his brother.   The timber for their first log hut was cut two or three miles up Flat River and floated down by the help of Indians, who were always friendly to those who used them well.

A tract of land lying on the east side of Flat River was set apart as university lands.   In 1836 Luther Lincoln, from Grand Rapids, came and settled on a small lot of the university lands, and built a log house, which was afterwards occupied by Don A. Marvin as a tavern.

In 1837, Charles Newton, Matthew Patrich, Samuel P. Rolf, Ira A. Dawes, William Vandeusen and Mr. Francisco settled along the north side of Grand River, on the old Grand River Road, from two to five miles west of Flat River.   In 1839, William B. Lyon and Ransom Rolf settled on the same road, near those previously mentioned.

At the time of the sale of lands in this tract, the Indians attempted to enter and hold the lands they had been tilling under the pre-emption laws; but, as the agent knew nothing about whether the red man could hold land by these laws, the matter was referred to the general land office, and, while waiting the decisions, Philander Tracy attempted to gain possession by erecting a small hut thereon and sowing the field with oats, which were destroyed by the Indians. His papers, which had been granted, were afterwards revoked, and, although the decision was unfavorable to the Indians, they loaned money to a Frenchman, who entered it for them.

John B. Shear and some others came in the year 1844, and settled in or near the present village of Lowell. In December, 1847, C. S. Hooker, formerly of Connecticut, came from Saranac. He erected the first frame house in the township, which was also the first in Lowell. In 1847, Mr. Hooker erected the grist mill on the east side of Flat River. It was run by an over-shot water-wheel, water being brought by means of a race, a distance of about forty rods from the island in Flat River. In 1849, Mr. Hooker constructed the dam across the river just below Bridge street.

The Lowell Postoffice was established about the year 1848, and took its name from the township, which was organized about the same time. The new village was called Lowell because of its prospects in a manufacturing point. The first village officers were: C. S. Hooker, President; C. A. Blake, Recorder; J. Chapman, Marshal; C. Hunt, Assessor; Wm. W. Hatch, J. B. Shear and A. Peck, Trustees.

Within the last few years Lowell has become a large

manufacturing and commercial mart. Its citizens are very enterprising, and many of its factories and business houses will compare favorably with those of Detroit.

CHAPTER XVIII.

EARLY SETTLEMENT OF NELSON, OAKFIELD, PLAINFIELD, SOLON AND SPARTA.

NELSON township is one of the northern tier. Twenty years ago this township was an unbroken wilderness, where wild animals made their homes.

In 1851, Wm. H. Bailey came and settled in Nelson. Mr. John S. Jones moved into the township during the same year, and is said to have been the second settler, and among those who followed were John M. Towns, Josiah Towns, N. R. Hill, D. B. Stout, H. M. Staunton, George Stout, Andrew Stout, Raleigh Smith, Samuel Punches, Joseph N. Clark, A. S. Tindell, J. N. Tindell, John Dean, Elisha Dean, H. D. Streter, Thomas Almy, Mr. Ream, and his two sons, Bradford Baily, and Joseph Wood.

Nelson was organized as a township on the 13th day

---

of October, 1854, and the first township election was held at the house of Chas. H. Leake, on the first Monday of April, 1855.

Oakfield was first settled in 1838, Wm. R. Davis being the pioneer of civilization. There seems to have been no one save himself and family to break the solitude of the wilderness till June, 1839, when Mr. Isaac Tower, Stephen S. Tower and William Thornton came with their families and settled near Mr. Davis. These were the only settlers till 1842, when Thomas Crinion and David J. Gilbert located on sections eighteen and nineteen, respectively. Then followed S. Ashley, Henry McArthur, Giles McArthur, Errie McArthur, Maurice Hart, M. W. Mack, John Davis, Levi White, James Eletley, Wm. Peterson and Benjamin Potter.

The first town meeting in Oakfield was held in April, 1849, at a little school house on section twenty-nine. This was the first school house in the town. The log cabin was replaced in 1852 by a frame structure of respectable size and appearance, and is still known as the White Swan School.

In Oakfield, pioneer life has passed almost entirely away, first-class schools are located in every settlement, and a goodly number of churches are handsomely supported. There are several mills on Wabassis Creek, all doing a profitable business. The first saw-mill in the township was built by John Davis, in 1846. It was located on Beaver Dam Creek. Three times it was swept into ruins by the freshets, and as often repaired or rebuilt by its persevering owner.

Paris is next to the oldest township in the county. As early as 1833, Barney Burton, Edward Guild, Joel

Guild, Danield Guild and James Vanderpool located within its present limits. Among the early settlers who followed were Jacob and Minor Patterson, James Patterson, O. Spaulding, P. Brown, N. Carleton, Hiram H. Allen, DeWitt Shoemaker, Clinton Shoemaker, Robert Shoemaker, Alom H. Wansey, J. Wansey, James Bollard, Stephen Hinsdill, A. Laraway, and Robert Barr.

The trials and hardships endured by the pioneers of those days seems to have been unusual. Nearly all of the settlers were poor, and the lot of some was peculiarly distressing. During 1837, or the "wild cat" times, many of the settlers endured untold hardships. Only a few of them had any considerable part of their farms cleared, and a still smaller part cultivated, and consequently were obliged to buy their provisions. Those who had been in the county longer and had larger improvements, raised a few bushels of wheat more than was required for their own use, but they could sell it neither for money nor for groceries.

While wheat was selling for only fifty cents a bushel, flour was selling for $15 and $20 a barrel, pork, $36 a

---

barrel, potatoes $2 per bushel, and butter fifty cents per pound.

Mr. Burton built the first log house in Paris, and erected the first barn in the county. He also erected the first frame house in the township. When Mr. Burton was on his way from Gull Prairie, one night in pioneer times, he and his few companions halted as usual, spancled their horses and took their rest. In the morning the horses belonging to Mr. Burton were not to be found, so he started in search of them. He wandered about in the thick woods for several hours without success, and finally turned about with the intention of re turning to the camp. He traveled until the sun was low in the west, and no camp could be found. Night came on, and he rested himself, a lost man in a dense forest. He spent the second day the same as the first, but on third he came out to the settlement of Ada. Thence he proceeded to Grand Rapids, where he found the settlers considerably excited over his disappearance. Mr. Campau had already dispatched several Indians in the direction he supposed he would be, to search for him.

At one time in the winter of 1835, the cries of what was supposed to be a man were heard in the vicinity of Mr. Burton's residence. He was answered, horns were blown, and other noises made to attract his attention, with no result. About the same time a grey horse came to the residence of A. Laraway, not many miles away, which none of the settlers claimed. Early in the spring a skeleton was found on what is now called the Penny Property, in Paris. Its appearance indicated that death had taken place some months previous. A few dollars in money, a watch and some papers were found on his person, the latter indicating that his name was Moore. Nothing further was ever ascertained in regard to the matter. He probably lost his way in the pathless woods, wandered about for several days, perhaps lost his horse, and starved to death; or, overcome with weariness, sank down to rest and perished by the excessive cold.

I might go on with incidents such as this in the history of Paris, but the want of space forbids.

Plainfield was first settled in 1837. It was named for the many plains within its borders.

Its first township meeting to complete its organization was held in April, 1838, at a rude log school house on section 23.

The township is well watered by the Grand and Rouge rivers and Mill Creek. The first mill was erected in 1840 by G. H. Gordon. It had a grist mill attached, and there the Indians and settlers carried their corn to be ground.

Among the early settlers of Plainfield I will mention Geo. Miller, Jas. Clark, Thos. Friant, W. Dexter, C. Friant, Z. Whitney, G. H. Gordon, Daniel North, Samuel Post, Jacob Post, Samuel Gross and Chester Wilson.

The first family on the ground was that of Mr. Geo. Miller, and the deprivations which fell to their share was the common lot of all who came to make a home in the wilds of Michigan at that day. Grand River was the only thoroughfare and means of communication with the outside world, hence the settlers depended mainly on what they raised, and their own ingenuity to prepare it for food. Pork, if imported, was $60 a barrel. The nearest flouring mill was sixty miles away, and the bread eaten in the family of Mr. Miller, for eighteen months. was ground in a coffee mill.

In 1838 the lands, although being surveyed and rapidly located, were not in the market, and it was no uncommon thing to see white men and Indians tilling corn in the same fields together. But in the fall of 1839 the great land sale came off, when the settlers secured their claims and the red man vanished from the scene.

Solon township lies in the north part of the county. It was first settled in 1854. J. M. Rounds and Mr. Beals were the first settlers, but were soon followed by John and Martin Hicks, Robbins Hicks and many others. The township was attached to Algoma until 1857, when it was organized into a separate town under the name of Solon. The first annual meeting was held at the house of Walker Rose, and the following officers were elected: Edward Jewell, Supervisor; John E. Roys, Clerk; John D. Watkins, Treasurer; Andrew Fluent, M. Robinson and Obidah Smith, Justices of the Peace.

This township is well watered, is being rapidly filled

---

up with enterprising settlers, and is fast increasing in wealth and importance.

Sparta is one of the northern tier of townships, and was first settled in 1844 by Lyman Smith, Norman and Edwin Cummings, who erected small shanties and began pioneer life with its usual hardships.

Soon after Lewis W. Pardy came, bringing his family, and erected a log house, and in 1845 Joseph English followed with his family. Thus the settlement began and continued, until the wilderness disappeared to give place to civilization and industry. Sparta is now a flourishing township, containing several villages and many enterprising citizens.

CHAPTER XIX.

EARLY SETTLEMENT OF SPENCER, WYOMING, WALKER, VERGENNES AND TYRONE.

SPENCER township is situated in the northeast corner of the county, and was first invaded by an old trapper by the name of Lincoln. He had a shanty on the bank of the lake of that name, and there he lived alone for a number of years.

The first regular settler was Cyrus B. Thomas, who located in the summer of 1846. The second settler was Henry Stroup, who located in January, 1848. M. B. Hatch came in 1853, and E. B. Cowles, B. G. Parks, Jacob Van Zandt, Wm. H. Hewitt, Wm. T. Parshall and Daniel Hastings followed. In a short time the township became well settled and soon began to show signs of rapid improvement.

The first township election was held in 1861.

Tyrone is the northwest corner township of Kent

county. It was first settled in 1849 by Mrs. Louisa Scott and family, who went in to board workmen on the State Road then being made on the west line of this township. In 1850 Lot Ferguson settled about one mile further on the road, where the Casnovia House afterwards stood.

In 1852 Jacob Smith and Harlon Jackson settled one mile east of the State Road, on the present road from Cedar Springs to Muskegon. In the following year John Thompson came into the same neighborhood, with Jos. Kies.

In 1855 other settlers came in, and soon the township became quite well settled by enterprising citizens, who have succeeded in improving the town and enriching themselves.

The township was, for some time, attached to Sparta, but in 1855 it was organized as a separate town under the name of Tyrone, the first annual meeting having been held at the only school house in the place, which stood near Mrs. Scott's residence.

Tyrone has now become a prosperous and thickly set-

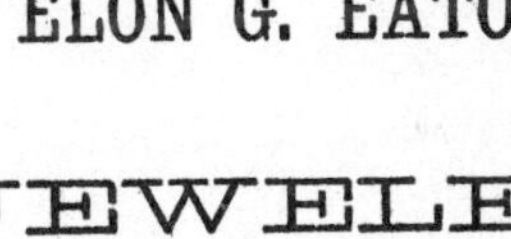

ELON G. EATON,

JEWELER

No. 7 CANAL ST.,

GRAND RAPIDS, - MICH.

tled town.   Within the township are several thrifty villages.   Excellent school houses have been erected and every improvement made necessary to make the homes of the residents comfortable.

Vergennes lies east of Ada. and was first settled by S. Hodges in 1836. It was organized under a separate town government in 1838, when there were only nineteen families in the township. For several years the farmers had to carry their grists to Ionia, to Grandville or to Kalamazoo to be ground.   At this time the township was comparatively an unbroken wilderness. Grand Rapids could boast of but half a score of poorly furnished houses and only two stores, those of Louis Campau and Mr. Watson.

Following is a list of the early settlers of Vergennes: S. S. Fallass, J. W. Fallass, L. Robinson, T. I. Daniels, James Wells, A. R. Hoag, S. Hodges, J. G. Fox, W. P. Perrin, A. Rogers, A. K. Shaw, E. Foster, N. Godfroy, A. Hodges, E. Walker, C. Misner, M. Lyon, B. Fairchild, J. Branagan and A. Vandeusen.

The record of this township is similar to that of the others. Its settlers had all the hardships of pioneer life, but in due time these difficulties gave way under the pressing progress of civilization and commerce. The wilderness was soon converted into fine farms, and mills were erected on the several streams ; school houses were erected, villages incorporated and commerce encouraged. Vergennes is now one of the most prosperous townships in Michigan.

Walker, one of the western tier of townships, was first settled by Samuel White in 1836.   Mr. White built the first frame barn west of Grand River, and soon after erected a saw mill on Indian Creek. Later in the same year Mr. White was joined by Jesse Smith and a Frenchman named John J. Nardin, who came and settled in the township. The following persons followed to complete the early settlement: Henry Helmka, Wm. W. Anderson, Joseph Denton, John Hogadone, Harvey Monroe, John Harrington, Patrick O'Brien, Stephen O'Brien, Jas. Murray and the Edison family. Many others followed at an early day.

The first township meeting was held in April, 1838, at the Mission School House. The records indicate that this was the only school house then in the township.

In 1838 emigration had fairly set in, and in a few years the place was thickly settled. All the settlers were enterprising, hard working men, and their energies were not exerted in vain. Walker has now become one of the best improved townships in Kent county, and promises a prosperous future. School houses have been erected in every school district in the town, and mills and manufacturing establishments have been put up with satisfactory results.

Wyoming is one of the western tier of townships of Kent county. It was first settled by Mr. David Tucker, G. H. Gordon, Luther Lincoln, Jos. B. Copeland, Hiram Jenison, William R. Godwin, J. T. Chubb, M. Roys, Henry West, R. Britton, J. C. Abel, E. P. Walker, A. Bryant, Joseph McCarthy and others.

In 1834 G. H. Gordon built a saw mill on section seventeen, and soon after other mills were erected. This was the beginning of enterprise in Wyoming, and it has been steadily kept up to the present day.

The existence of plaster in this township is probably one reason for its rapid settlement and great enterprise.

The first mill for grinding plaster was built in the winter of 1840 by Mr. Daniel Ball, of Grand Rapids.

CHAPTER XX.

GRAND RAPIDS IN 1846 AND IN 1874—THE GROWTH OF THE VALLEY CITY.

HAVING briefly traced some of the incidents in the early settlement of the several townships in Kent county, we will now return to the city of Grand Rapids. In our mention of the several towns, however, we must be excused for not giving the growth of each in detail, since the limits of this little work will not admit of anything more than a partial history of the county.

To say that Grand Rapids city has had a rapid growth in all her industries, and that everything in her present condition combines to demonstrate her future greatness, is truly within reason. That the city will, in time, contain a population almost equal to Detroit there can be but little doubt, and that it will always maintain a second position among the cities of Michigan, no person acquainted with the advantages of the location and the great enterprise of the citizens of the Grand River Valley, will dispute.

If we desire to see what the growth of the city has been, let us take a view of it in 1846, only twenty-seven years ago. Then, forty acres was about the extent of the place. Division street might be said to bound civilization on the east, Monroe street on the south, Bridge street on the north, and the river on the west. There were scattered buildings only outside of those limits. A wing dam ran half way across the river, and furnished water power for three saw mills, two grist mills, and some minor works. Irving Hall, Faneul Hall, Commercial Block, Backus Block, and Pierce's Franklin Block were the principal stores, the last two mentioned being nearly " out of town." St. Claire's store, where Luce's Hall now is, was the business stand farthest up Monroe street. Canal street was a mud hole from one end to the other, and a two-foot side walk, supported by posts, kept the pedestrians out of the mud. This street has since been filled in from five to ten feet. Where Fitch & Raymond's carriage shop was afterwards built, and around there, was a fine, musical frog-pond. The stumps were in the street and the houses were all one story. The only communication with the outside world, besides the river and lakes, was by the Battle Creek stage. People came to church with ox teams. There were no fashionables, people dressed plain and nearly all had the ague. Every cow could boast a bell, and thus the little town was amply supplied with music. Wood was one dollar a cord, wheat fifty cents a bushel, corn twenty-five cents, venison one-half cent a pound, pork and beef three cents.

At this time Mr. Ballard was preaching in the Congregational Church, and got his living by farming. The Catholics used a dwelling house for a chapel. Such was Grand Rapids in 1846.

But to-day Grand Rapids is a large and prosperous city, with a population of nearly twenty-five thousand, among whom are some of the most enterprising men in the Northwest.

To avoid writing in a general way I will take up the several institutions of the city separately. By this means the reader may become acquainted with the growth and history of the city more definitely. In this I shall make no distinction as to the merits of the several institutions noticed. Churches, manufacturing establishments, schools and banks, commercial houses and libraries, or whatever have contributed to the growth of the city, or by their own growth and development have become important interests in the city, will be taken up without regard to any particular order.

CHAPTER XXI.

GRAND RAPIDS COMMERCIAL COLLEGE—ENTERPRISE OF PROF. SWENSBERG—THE IMPORTANCE AND EXCELLENCE OF THE COLLEGE.

IF WE except the public schools, there is, perhaps, no other institution in Grand Rapids of so much value to the city and its citizens, at this particular period, as the Grand Rapids Commercial College and Telegraphic Institute. If we speak in reference to other colleges of a similar course of study, we should say that, for thoroughness and appointments, it is the best in America. The author of this little work has had an extensive acquaintance with business colleges, both in the Eastern and Northwestern States, and is now able to say, with truthfulness, to the citizens of Grand Rapids, that they can justly boast of having the most advanced, the most elevated and best conducted Commercial College in the United States. In short, Prof. C. G. Swensberg, the principal of the institution, has raised it so far above the ordinary business colleges of the country as to convince all who become acquainted with the course of study pursued at his college that the science of business is equal, in point of importance and accomplishment, to any art or science generally classed among the "higher studies." Many have an idea that persons attend a commercial college merely to study book-keeping.   This is a mistake. It is not so, at least, with those who attend the Grand Rapids College. The discipline and course of study through which they have to pass, under the constant and thorough conduct of Prof. Swensberg, in point of mathematical and commercial science and moral training, is equal to a course of study in many of the regular colleges.

Only a few days ago it was my pleasure to listen to the second lecture of the law course, delivered before the students of this college by Hon. H. M. Look. The discourse was alike instructive and interesting, and was scarcely less an exercise in eloquence than commercial law.

The reputation of this college has become almost national, and its many students have gathered from nearly half the States of the Union, leaving the business colleges in their own neighborhood, and passing others on the way, to obtain the superior advantages offered in the Commercial College of Grand Rapids. This is alike flattering to Prof. Swensberg and to the citizens of Grand Rapids.

Mr. Henry S. Chubb, Secretary of the Northern Michigan Agricultural and Mechanical Society, in writing a sketch of the principal institutions of Grand Rapids, makes the following appropriate remarks concerning this college and its principal .

"Prof. Swensberg, Principal of this College, has long held a high place in the esteem of the people, especially the young people, of Grand Rapids, from the fact that his influence has been exerted for their especial good. He has shown a genuine interest in their welfare, not merely in insisting on their perfection in the arts of penmanship and book-keeping, to which he is especially devoted, but in their general character and conduct. Many a now prosperous business man looks back with gratitude to the period when, under Prof. Swensberg's instruction, he imbibed those honorable principles which are recognized among all men as the foundation of good citizenship and commercial prosperity. How much the enterprise, the spirit and integrity of the city, is owing to the influence and power of the Commercial College, enforced by the example of its ever zealous Principal, can never be told or realized. Suffice it to say, the influence is exerted just at the period when young people are most sensitive; and being exerted for a continuous period, has the best possible effect. The students, finding immediate and profitable employment after graduating, the effect on the business functions of the city soon become apparent.

The business course consists of book-keeping, commercial law, commercial arithmetic, business correspondence, composition, orthography and penmanship.

Book-keeping is taught in a thorough and scientific manner, in all its various forms, commencing first with the most simple transactions from which to make up and arrange sets of books, and gradually increasing to the most difficult that can occur in any department of trade or commerce.

Each student is required to open, write up and close over forty different sets of books, with particular forms and illustrations, adapted to every kind of business ; and in connection with these sets, the student is also required to write up for rigid inspection all drafts, notes, bills of exchange, receipts, orders, checks, bills, accounts current, account sales, bills of lading, bonds, contracts, leases, general averages, statements, letters—in short, all papers in any way connected with the business.

The methods of partnership, settlements, business correspondence and information concerning all the methods of varied business transactions and the fundamental principles on which business is or should be transacted, are taught in the most thorough manner, so that the pupil graduates with a practical knowledge which fits him to enter the actual duties of life without the embarrassment usually incident to beginners.

German, French, Phonography and Telegraphing are all taught, if desired, and students are fitted for any particular line of business."

Prof. C. G. Swensberg, while devoting his time and attention to his duties as Principal of the Commercial College, does not fail to lend his influence and means to encourage other enterprises. He is a stock-holder in several manufacturing enterprises, and was for many years closely and honorably identified with almost every movement of importance in the city. He has contributed not a little to the success of the Young Men's Christian Association, of Grand Rapids, having served in the capacity of Secretary and Vice-President of the Association for several years, and on different committees.

CHAPTER XXII.

Manufacturing Establishments—Enterprise of James M. and Ezra T. Nelson—Some Incidents of their Pioneer Life—Success of Mr. E. Matter—The Establishment of Nelson, Matter & Co.

One of the oldest, largest and best appointed furniture manufactories in the Northwestern States is that owned and conducted by Messrs. Nelson, Matter & Co , at Grand Rapids. It was established in 1855 by Hon. C. C. Comstock, who conducted it alone until 1863, when he was joined by the Messrs. Nelson Brothers, who have been honorably identified with the early settlement of the Grand River Valley.

It is not too much to say that this extensive factory was the pioneer institution of the kind at the Rapids, and that all those which have sprung up after it owe their great success not a little to the efforts of this firm. It is always easier to follow in the tracks of another through a pathless forest than to work out one's own course by the aid of our own unaided ingenuity. So it is also easier to establish and succeed in a new enterprise when guided by the land marks of another. When this factory was first started it was completely an experiment, and it required an abiding faith in the future growth of Grand Rapids to induce one to embark in it. Such was the faith of Mr. Comstock and the Nelson Brothers, and time alone has developed how keen and penetrating was their foresight. No other person's means had been invested to demonstrate the feasibility of the plan ; no end had been accomplished that in any way demonstrated its propriety, and few were the signs and faint the hopes for the future greatness of the Valley City. Grand Rapids was comparatively a mud hole; its inhabitants were mostly French—in short, there was nothing in the place which gave the sound of American enterprise. A miserable and declining traffic with a few tribes of wretched Indians inadequately supported the French population, whose wonder and disapproval were not a little excited at the conduct of the few "Yankee" pioneers, who, with keen axes upon their shoulders, marched bravely into the depths of the forest, building their hopes upon a sound faith in the future development of the whole Northwest.

This is a grand view, and needs only to be painted in dim colors to please those old pioneers who still live to enjoy what they then dilligently hoped for. Look at the enterprising man of 1836, who leaves his eastern home and penetrates the wilds of the western forests. When he can no longer travel by the jolting stage, and when there is no longer any road or trail by which to complete his journey, he completes the distance by cutting his way, until, steadily progressing day after day and week after week, he finds himself shut out from civilization, encompassed by a desolating forest, and, perhaps, a family depending upon him for support. He toils on with his only weapon, by which the majestic trees were made to bow their lofty tops to the ground. Soon his little hut begins to assume shapely proportions, and now the shivering wife and children, who have all this time warmed themselves by a log fire, gladly retreat within the log enclosure, which, after all, is but a poor excuse for a shelter. The December storms beat through the open windows or the large openings between the logs, but still the warm heart of the pioneer beats. on, and the lonely family forget their sorrows as they listen to his hopeful words.

Such was the picture of life in the valley of the Grand River when James M. and Ezra T. Nelson came to Kent, the principal town for miles and miles around. It contained about half a dozen houses, five or six hundred Indians, a few Indian traders, a mission house, a blacksmith shop, one or two stores, no streets except in an imaginary point—in fact nothing but a few miserable huts in a lonely wilderness.

But they were not discouraged. Believing that in a near future a large and prosperous city would grow up at the head of navigation on the Grand River, they invested their means in Kent property and began to share the common lot of the pioneer

Being of a mercantile turn of mind, they bought out Mr. James Lyman, or Messrs. Lyman & Dwight, in order to get a store, and commenced business. Soon after Mr. James M. Nelson purchased a lot in the Kent plat and began preparation for building a house. He supplied Mr. Barney Burton with means to erect a saw mill on Mill Creek, and sent men into the lumber woods. The first raft of logs ever brought down the Grand River belonged to Mr. Nelson. The mill was put into operation and the lumber for the proposed house was soon provided and the building erected.

Mr. Jas. M. Nelson lumbered on the river for nearly twelve years with his brother, Ezra T. Nelson, built several mills, and prosecuted a large and profitable buiness. He soon became honorably identified with the business and political interests of the town. He was Postmaster of the town four years, and Supervisor and Overseer of the Poor until the city was organized, when he retired from public life in order to give his time more unreservedly to business.   He was also active in promoting the educational interests of the city, having built the old Union School House and purcha ed the property on which it stood.   His influence was also exerted for the promotion and welfare of the city churches, especially those of the Episcopal denomination.   Upon the organization of the city government he was unanimously nominated for the first Mayor of Grand Rapids, and would have been elected without any considerable opposition had he not declined the honors and responsibilities of the office.

As I have already mentioned, Mr. James M. and Ezra T. Nelson purchased a half interest in the furniture factory of Hon. C. C. Comstock, in 1863. The firm was then called Comstock, Nelson & Co. In 1865, T. A. Comstock, M. G. Colson and James A. Pugh purchased Mr. C. C. Comstock's interest, and the firm name was changed to Nelson, Comstock & Co.   The business was successfully continued by this firm until 1870, when Mr. E. Matter purchased Mr. T. A. Comstock's interest, changing the firm name to Nelson, Matter & Co., which style it still retains.   In February, 1872, Mr. Stephen S. Gay purchased Mr. Colson's interest, the firm continuing under the same name.   In 1871 the firm purchased the interest of James A. Pugh.

Mr. E. Matter, who became a member of this firm in 1870, came to Grand Rapids in 1855.   After clerking a short time in a boot and shoe house, he engaged as foreman of C. C. Comstock's factory—the same concern in which he afterwards became a leading partner.   He afterwards joined Julius Berkey in the manufacture of furniture, and as we have seen, became a partner with the Nelsons, under the firm name of Nelson, Matter & Co.

Mr. Matter has thus come up from small beginning to a position of leading importance.   Beginning in Grand Rapids in 1855, without any capital, he has persevered skillfully, until he has accumulated an independent fortune—the result of his great energy and faultless integrity.

The firm of Nelson, Matter & Co. is, perhaps, one of the wealthiest, or, to use a business phrase, "soundest" concern in Grand Rapids.   It is not improbable that the recent financial panic has considerably interfered with their business, but it has in no way shaken the solid foundation on which they stand.   They represent an invested capital of over $300,000, and sell annually over $200,000 worth of furniture.   These immense sales extend into nearly all the States, and into the whole Northwest.

Their factory, which is located on the corner of Lyon and Lock streets, in the very heart of the city, is supplied with ample steam power, and is the most complete and best appointed establishment in Grand Rapids. It is a five-story brick, including a basement, 70x160 feet, and has a capacity for over two hundred workmen.

The visitor's eye is first captivated by the steam engine, boilers, pumps, and extensive steam works. These are located in the rear of the factory, where, beneath them, exists a large reservoir, carried in from the canal, for the purpose of supplying the boilers with water. The immense boilers are heated by furnaces which are supplied with fuel in a peculiar manner. The shavings are carried from the planing and molding machines by means of suction pipes to the doors of the furnaces, so that when the factory is running to its fullest capacity, it is almost self-sustaining in point of fuel.

The engine is an immense one, of 200 horse power, which supplies its own strength by pumping the water from the reservoir below into a large tank, where it is met and heated by the exhaust steam, and from there pumped into the boiler. This is a great improvement over pumping cold water into steam boilers, is a great saving of fuel, and is a valuable prevention against accidents. It would require half a volume to give anything like a detailed account of how the steam is conducted through the building for heating purposes, and I shall be contented with saying that it is the most perfect, and withal, the most interesting contrivance in the country.

There are three entrances to the main floor of the factory—one from Lyon street, one from Lock street, and one from the river. In each of these entrances an iron track is laid, upon which trucks are run in and out, loaded with lumber or stock, by steam power. There is a turn-table in the center of the building, so that the trucks can be removed from one track to another, as convenience may require.

On this floor the lumber is subjected to the cross-cutters and rippers, and is cut into drawer fronts, sides, table tops, pieces for dressing cases, etc. It is also planed on this floor, and is then sent to the second floor, where are located the band and jig saws, the molders, borers, joiners, turning lathes, etc. Here they "machine" the stock, and the performance is indeed an interesting one. There is no better amusement than to stand by one of the molders when in operation, or to watch the intricate circles of the band and jig saws. This floor presents a busy scene. Every machine is running with full velocity, and the rough, unshapely stock is converted into beautiful ornaments as if by the power of magic.

The work is next carried, by the elevator, to the third and fourth floors, where it goes into the hands of the workmen at the benches and is put together. Here it begins to take the shape of furniture. The carving and designing department is located here, and is under the efficient supervision of James F. Donnelly.

On the opposite side of Lock street are located the warehouses, which are always filled with excellent furniture af all kinds, ready for shipment. One of these warehouses has a frontage on Lyon street and the other on Huron street. They are connected with each other and to the factory by means of bridges.

A very important part of this establishment is the lumber yard, which is located on Kent street. Here is to be found over 1,000,000 feet of lumber. The drying kiln is always full, and thus the stock is well seasoned before going into the factory.

The exposition rooms, Nos. 33, 35 and 37 Canal street, is a building 54x80 feet, three stories above the basement. In this building are located the offices, show-rooms, parlor, finding and trimming departments.

Nelson, Matter & Co. make the largest variety of furniture of any house in Grand Rapids—chamber, parlor, dining room and office furniture, are, however, specialties. Their chamber suites are among the best manufactured, ranging from the plainest to the most elegant and costly.

They find a ready market for their goods, both east, south and west, and their immense trade is annually increasing.

CHAPTER XXIII.

THE GROWTH OF GRAND RAPIDS—ITS RAILROADS, CHURCHES, SCHOOLS, BUILDINGS, AND VARIOUS INSTITUTIONS.

SINCE the close of the war of the rebellion in 1865, perhaps no city of its size in the United States has had a more rapid and substantial growth than Grand Rapids. The "Illustrated History of Michigan," recently compiled by the author of this work, closes its review of Grand Rapids with these paragraphs:

"There are now three daily newspapers, the *Democrat*, *Eagle* and *Times*, representing the Democratic and Republican parties, and the latter Independent. There are also soveral weekly papers, one of which is printed exclusively in the Holland language. There are twenty-three organized churches, and some of the edifices are of a superior kind in point of architectural design. The First Congregational is a gothic building, elegant in finish, costing $65,000. St. Marks, Episcopal, one of the oldest church edifices in the city, has lately been enlarged and improved at a cost of $30,000, and is one of the largest gothic edifices west of Detroit in Michigan, worth $60,000. The First Methodist has a fine structure in the Roman style, elaborately finished and furnished, costing $45,000. The Baptist Society have erected a very costly gothic church which is a superb contribution to the many beautiful houses of worship in the city, its estimated cost being $80,000. The First Presbyterians have a very fine house on the west side, which cost $30,000. The Methodists have also, in this locality, a really handsome gothic church, containing in its tower the largest bell in the city and a fine clock; cost, $40,000. The Roman Catholics have a handsome gothic church built and are occupying it, which cost $43,000, and have another building, for a German congregation, at an expense of $60,000. The Episcopalians have in addition to the parent church—St. Mark's —three chapels, while the two Holland churches have

large and finely appointed edifices completed, one costing $35,000.   The Westminster Presbyterian Society has
a very nice church edifice on the east side, while the
Dutch Reformed congregation is taking steps to build a
$25,000 house.   The old Catholic church of St. Andrew
has been disposed of, and plans for a $100,000 cathedral
are now being perfected.   The Universalists have a very
pretty and well finished and furnished church.

"The manufacturing interests of Grand Rapids are
large and rapidly increasing.   Generally, they may be
summed up in three flouring, one woolen, fifteen saw,
four plaster and other mills, three furnaces, two boiler
factories, four tanneries, six large furniture manufactories and a dozen smaller ones, three extensive chair factories, ten large cooper shops, six extensive carriage
manufactories, ten wagon shops, one chemical works,
three pail and bucket factories, one clothes pin factory
one gypsum ornament manufactory, several sash, door
and blind shops, two saw manufactories, three marble
and stone yards, one brush factory, Waters' patent barrel factory, two hub factories, two manufactories of
farming implements, one faucet manufactory ; in fact,
almost everything that can be made from wood has a
manufactory in this city.   Fanning mills, milk safes and
such like useful articles are extensively fabricated, and
all these varied industries—large numbers of which we
have not attempted to enumerate—furnish employment
for an army of mechanics, artisans and laborers, who are
paid weekly for their skill and efforts in developing
the city's resources.

" Upon either side of Grand River is a canal, which
furnishes a vast amount of power for propelling the ma-

chinery incident to the manufacturing enterprises of the place, the descent in the river over the rapids producing a head and fall of sixteen feet; yet it is safe to say that fully one-half of the whole power used in the various departments of mechanical effort in the city is made from steam.

"At this time of writing six railroads are in operation, under control of some of the most extensive corporations in the country, sending out and receiving daily the passengers upon thirty trains of cars, while the immense freighting business incident to the lumber, plaster and manufacturing interests are indeed great. . A street railway from the Detroit and Milwaukee Railroad has long been in operation, running through Leonard, Canal, Monroe and Fulton streets, and when continued to the Fair Grounds, will be a great source of great convenience.

This year (1873) upwards of three hundred buildings of all kinds, including forty stores, are in process of erection, and it is one of the strong points of the resources of Grand Rapids that all the stone for paving or building, and fine yellow brick, as good as those made in Milwaukee, with lime, Plaster of Paris, stucco and sand, are found within the corporation, while the country immediately north abounds with the best of pine, cedar, beech, maple, and other merchantable woods out of which lumber is made. With the exception of paint, nails, and gas piping, the materials for an entire ordinary dwelling are to be found in the city, the product of the county.

"The public schools of the city are as good as the best in the State, and comprise one Union or High school and eight ward schools, all under control of a Board of Education, consisting of two members from each ward, with the Mayor, who are elected by the people. The buildings occupied for school purposes are mostly of brick, and of attractive design, with good play grounds. There is a City Library of upwards of 6,000 volumes, supported by fines, the result of violated ordinances; also, a "Kent Scientific Institute," which has one of the most valuable collections of specimens, minerals, fossils, etc., to be found in the State, and one which has attracted considerable attention from scientists.

"The Young Men's Christian Association is in a very flourishing state, and its organization has not only been efficient but exceedingly useful in the line of its christian duty and quiet charities. 'St. Mark's Home' is a hospital under the immediate control of some ladies of St. Mark's church, and has proved itself of great benefit to many, as its doors are open to all, without distinction of creed. The charges for board and care are just sufficient to cover actual cost, for such as can pay, and to such as cannot and are worthy, no charge is made.

"'The Union Benevolent Society' is another charitable hospital, of a more enlarged character, which has been in existence for upwards of fifteen years. It is managed by ladies and gentlemen selected from the various Protestant organizations, and is incorporated. Having an eligible and and admirably located lot, steps are now being taken towards the erection of a suitable building to accommodato their rapidly increasing wants.

" This city is the acknowledged metropolis of western and northwestern Michigan.   Its location is one of admitted beauty, having a rare variety of hill and dale for landscape, while it is noted for its elegant residences, suburban villas, fine business blocks, and the air of ac tivity and thrift which characterizes so many of our western towns.   The United States have decided to erect a suitable public building here for its District Courts, Pension Office, U. S. Marshal's Office, Collector, Post-office, etc., etc., and has ordered a free postal delivery system, in accordance with a law of Congress passed at its last session.   It should be added that during the season of navigation boats ply regularly on the Grand River to Grand Haven, and a large amount of business is transacted along the shores, which are dotted with thriving villages.

" The traveling public are well cared for in several hotels, which are well kept, though the rapid increase of population and the influx of strangers, attracted by the wide-spread notoriety of the place for business, demand increased facilities in this line, and steps are being taken towards the erection of more hotel room.   There are two free bridges and one toll bridge spanning the river— which is 900 feet wide—also two railroad bridges.   The wholesale business of Grand Rapids in groceries, boots and shoes, dry goods, hardware and manufactured articles from wood, is large and rapidly increasing. Several of its streets are paved with stone, while wooden pavements are now coming into general use. Owing to the hilly nature of a large part of the city plat and the necessity of much filling near the river, on the east side, the grading and leveling of streets has been a costly undertaking, but it has been accomplished during the ten years past at an outlay of nearly a hundred thousand dollars per annum. The ground forming the plat on the west side is very level, and calculated for a large city, backed and skirted as it is by very bold and delightful bluffs. Situated as Grand Rapids is, in the vicinity of a splendid farming, fruit, wool raising and well wooded country, it must continue to increase in wealth, population and intelligence, and remain in the future, as it is now, the second city of Michigan, and through its various institutions and enterprise of a business, religious and social nature, must do no small share in moulding the thought and giving tone and direction to the population which is rapidly filling up the great country north as far as Mackinaw, and west to the shore of Lake Michigan."

CHAPTER XXIV.

The Buildings and Business Houses of Grand Rapids—Dry Goods House of Spring & Avery.

One of the largest and most successful dry goods houses in northwestern Michigan is that owned and conducted by Messrs. Spring & Avery, at Grand Rapids. This extensive establishment, which is now located in the new and beautiful Crawfor d Block, at the foot of

Monroe street, was first started in 1861, twelve years ago, on Canal street. During the first year the firm did a business of about $40,000, which has increased, year after year, until in 1873 their sales exceeded $300,000. This great increase of business is grandly significant of the rapid growth of the city, and, perpaps, has had not a little to do in promoting it. The firm continued their business on Canal street for one winter, and then removed to No. 48 Monroe street, where they remained, doing a successful business until the winter of 1873–4, when they removed to their new and elegant store at the foot of Monroe street. This is one of the finest interiors, being the best lighted and most completely appointed of any house in northwestern Michigan. It is four stories and a basement, each 44x100 feet, all of which are occupied by the business of Messrs. Spring & Avery. The basement is devoted to the wholesale trade, in which this firm are now doing a large and rapidly increasing business.

The main floor is devoted to the retailing of staple and fancy dry goods, cloths, shawls, etc. The second floor is

---

occupied by the high-priced carpets, such as Moquettes, Body Brussels, Axminsters, etc. This is, in itself, the largest carpet house in Grand River Valley, and for variety and fullness of stock, is quite equal to older eastern houses. The third floor is devoted to a cheaper grade of carpets, oil cloths, straw carpets, etc. This floor alone constitutes a very extensive carpet establishment, containing a very large and choice stock of all the cheaper carpets. The fourth floor is devoted to the manufacture of carpets for the retail trade.

Thus it will be seen that this extensive house is four-fold, or that it embraces four extensive floors, on each of which an active and profitable business is conducted.

That such an immense establishment should grow up in the short period of twelve years is not a little flattering to the prospects of this section. It bespeaks a healthy industry and a fast growing commerce for the Valley City.

Messrs. Henry Spring and Edward Avery, the members of this firm, are both residents of Grand Rapids of high reputation. In matters of business they have established an unshaken confidence in every person, thus enabling them to place the products of every market, both eastern and European, before their numerous patrons of Northwestern Michigan.

Their retail dry goods department, which is on the main floor, contains all the appointments known to the modern exposition room. The fixtures are of the most elegant kind, and the very large plate glass windows admit a volume of light that seems to enliven the whole aspect. The floor is divided into regular departments. On the right of the front entrance we have the domestic goods. Next come the flannels, linens, and lastly the cloths and casimeres. On the left we have the dress goods, extending in various grades a distance of nearly one hundred feet. First we find the cheaper grades, then they become higher and finer until we come to the silks, which include a splendid line of black and colored. Beyond this, still further on, are the cloaks and shawls, where, by the aid of large mirrors, the customer may test the effect and appearance of the many styles. In the centre of this floor we have first, as we enter, the fancy and staple notions, which embrace a complete variety. In the rear of this is the cashier's desk, and still beyond is the broad walnut staircase leading to the carpet department on the next floor. On the right of this is the private office of the firm.

I have no space here to enter into a description of the carpet department, but it will suffice to say that it is in itself a complete and extensive carpet house, containing the largest and most desirable stock of carpets in this section of the country.

In prosecuting this extensive business Messrs. Spring & Avery employ some thirty persons, clerks, book keepers, salesmen etc. Among their salesmen will be found not only the expert talker, but gentlemen—residents of Grand Rapids—who have established themselves in the confidence of their employers and in the favor and esteem of their patrons.

BERKEY & GAY FURNITURE CO.

NOT ALWAYS DOES SUCCESS crown the labors of the industrious, or prosperity attend the struggles of sobriety and integrity. In dangerous emulation of the rapid career of certain individuals who have risen to a sudden and spurious eminence, the passion to be rich in haste has driven many impatient business men through the intricate paths of tortuous and crooked speculation.

ATTRACTIVE AS ARE THE DAZZLING, though temporary, results of all such unstable and abortive schemes, a safer road to affluence and honor lies through the more tedious and toilsome walks of patient industry and economy.

THE VEGETABLE AND MINERAL RESOURCES of Michigan, as of other States, are presented freely to every man who chooses to avail himself of these treasures; and every aspirant for the honor and wealth resulting from well directed manufacture may reap a rich reward.

BUT DURING MANY YEARS sober application to business, within the limits of available capital, has been too frequently supplanted by crude and ill-considered projects, based wholly on chance and the uncertainties of the future.

ESPECIALLY NOTICEABLE has been this condition of affairs when new regions have been first occupied, and when the almost boundless profusion of natural wealth spread a most tempting attraction before the eyes of the incautious.

NOT UNIVERSALLY, however, was this spirit of unhealthy speculation exhibited; and not without gratification, and perhaps surprise, can Mr. Julius Berkey recall the retired and unobtrusive character of his earliest efforts as a manufacturer, or the limited range of his operations. The narrow accommodation then at his command is now only a recollection; but some models of his earliest work are still employed, and well maintain their place, even among the most improved manufactures of to-day. Limiting his efforts to the means actually at his command, yet slowly and surely reaching forward, as resources and opportunities accumulated, Mr. Berkey, in co-operation with his partners, laid the foundation of the extended and prosperous enterprise with which he is associated still.

A FEW CHANGES IN PARTNERSHIP have not impeded the steady advance of the firm in enterprise or energy, and so greatly did the business flourish and widen that the remaining proprietors, Mr. Julius Berkey and Mr. Geo. W. Gay, who joined the firm as early as 1866, merged their interests in a corporation during the year just closed.

THE NEW FIRM have commenced their corporate career with the advantage of many years of successful experience, and with a wide-spread reputation; and their capital is authorized by law to be extended to half a million of dollars.

AT THE OUTSET OF THESE OPERATIONS the prospects of an extensive furniture trade were not wholly bright; but experience has demonstrated that

young and vigorous enterprises can in time rival or surpass even much older institutions; and the furniture
manufactured in Grand Rapids is now in successful
competition with the productions of the longest established manufactories of the country, and the Berkey &
Gay Furniture Company stand second to none in solid
reputation.

THUS FROM A SLENDER COMMENCEMENT
has this eminent firm progressed to the high position it
now occupies; and at the present time a large factory
replete with the most approved machinery, some of it
constructed after Mr. Berkey's own designs; warehouses
loaded with specimens of the highest style of modern
furniture, and lumber yards filled with an immense supply of walnut and other valuable wood, are the substantial and enduring evidence that under divine Provi-
dence the prosperity of the firm has been created by
well directed economy.

THE SAME PRUDENT MANAGEMENT, which,
at the outset, resisted all temptations towards insecure
expansion, pervades the conduct of the business now,
and is a guarantee to all the patrons of the firm that the
prices of all articles offered for sale have not been inflated by careless purchases of material, or insufficient
attention to the details of construction.

PROSPERITY IN THE COURSE OF TRADE has
not obstructed the improvement of processes, or the
adoption of increased elegance of style and design ; and
the firm which did not curtail its expenses one hour during the recent exhausting and alarming panic, has afforded sufficient demonstration of the possession of high
business qualifications.

AT THE PRESENT TIME the operations of this firm extend throughout the largest portion of the United States; and even the comparatively unsettled regions of Utah, Colorado, Wyoming, Dacotah and Montana, as well as the older States, and the prosperous cities of San Francisco and Sacramento in California, are indebted to the enterprise of this firm for the possession of many of those elegancies of domestic decoration which add so largely to the comforts and refinements of life.

THE WAREROOMS of the Berkey & Gay Furniture Co., although spacious and occupying the larger portion of five extensive buildings, do not supply sufficient accommodation; but we may expect that ample provision in this behalf will be made as soon as possible, under the superintendence of the present Board of Directors.

JULIUS BERKEY, President.
GEO. W. GAY, Treasurer.
ARTHUR J. HOLT, Secretary.

TYLER, GRAHAM & CO.

This firm began the jobbing and wholesaleing of staple notions in Grand Rapids about five years ago, and meeting with great success they established, two years later, a branch of their house in Detroit at Nos. 145 and 147 Jefferson avenue. The Grand Rapids house is located on Pearl street, opposite Sweet's Hotel, and is one of the finest appointed business houses in the city.

This firm is now doing a very large wholesale business in the State of Michigan and in the northern parts of the States of Ohio and Indiana, with every prospect of a continuance of their rapidly expanding trade. The affairs of the two houses are conducted on a systematic basis well calculated to insure prosperity. The partners are Messrs. S. M. Tyler, W. L. Graham, A. E. Worden and A. B. Miner. Mr. S. M. Tyler attends to the buying for the Detroit house, and Mr. A. E. Worden for the Grand Rapids house, while the two other partners, Messrs. Graham and Miner, attend to the finances of the respective establishments.

They purchase their goods principally among eastern manufacturers, and are enabled to place them in the western market at very low figures. Messrs. Tyler and Worden are both experienced buyers, having had long connection with the manufacturers of their line of goods; and it is largely due to their energy and foresight that the wholesale market in Grand Rapids for staple notions, trimmings etc., affords all the advantages of the older eastern houses. Indeed, the growth and prosperity of this house is no small item in the commerce of the Valley City.

JAMES S. CROSBY & SON.

This is one of the most extensive insurance and real estate firms in Grand Rapids. Their record of successful business life in this city extends over a period of sixteen years, and with the progress and growth of the city their business has increased, step by step, until today they represent a long list of the best insurance companies in the world, and extend their real estate transactions over a large territory.

The business of the firm was first opened in Grand Rapids in 1858 by Mr. James S. Crosby. He conducted it successfully for five years, when, in 1863, he associated his son, Mr. Marian S. Crosby, with him as a partner, and from that period the firm has been known under the present style.   In their insurance department they now represent the following companies: The Liverpool and London and Globe, with a cash capital and assets of over $20,000,000; the North British and Mercantile, with assets of the United States branch exceeding $1,700,000; the Royal, of Liverpool, with assets reaching a trifle over $12,000,000; the Phœnix, of N. Y., with $2,000,000 assets; also, the Manhattan, the Irving, the Hoffman; the Orient, the Commerce and the Faneul Hall companies. To this list should be added the Traveler's and the Railway Passenger Insurance Companies, of Hartford.

Messrs. Crosby & Son, it will be seen by the above list, represent several of the most reliable insurance companies doing business in the United States.   All are familiar with the great advantages of the Liverpool and London and Globe.   The unlimited liability of its stockholders and its great promptness in discharging all claims recommend it in preference to many others.   In short, persons wishing to transact any business either in real estate or insurance will do well to patronize this firm.

CRAWFORD BROS.

Messrs. Frank and Alfred Crawford, two young and enterprising men, citizens of Grand Rapids, are entitled to a mention in this work.   They came to Grand Rapids about the time of the war, without means, but through great industry and, I should say, hard work, they have accumulated considerable wealth and won a reputation worth vastly more.   They began the grocery business about five years ago in Grand Rapids, with a capital of only one thousand dollars, but in that short period they have accomplished a great business feat. Their first store was located at the foot of Monroe street where their new block now stands, but they subsequently removed to their present location, No. 13 Pearl street.

They began the erection of the "Crawford Block" in May, 1873, and in December of the same year the building was completed and occupied by Messrs. Spring & Avery, the popular dry goods firm. This elegant building is composed of brick and stone, is 44x100 feet, with four stories and a basement, and is one of the handsomest and most serviceable buildings in the city. The building and lot is worth not less than $75,000, but it is not probable that it could be purchased for $80,000.

The growing business of Messrs. Crawford Bros. is larger to-day than ever before. They are doing a large wholesale trade, sending their goods into all parts of Northwestern Michigan, and in the retail trade they do as much business as any house in the city. Their store is always crowded, presenting a scene of busy activity, and the Messrs. Crawford are always there giving personal attention to their customers.

These gentlemen rank among the most industrious citizens of Grand Rapids, and their exertions in the past have been largely instrumental in promoting the growth and prosperity of the city. The new Crawford Block is a very good monument to their industry, and it speaks grandly to their praise.

Although they have already accumulated a competency, these gentlemen do not relax their energies. They are pushing forward, enlarging their business and keeping pace with the rapid growth of Grand Rapids.

The new Crawford Block is located in the very heart

of the city at the foot of Monroe street, and is a very valuable addition to the architectural beauty of the city. The entire building is admirably appointed. Broad staircases lead from one floor to the other, making the ascent easy and agreeable. In short, it is admirably adapted to the advanced interests of the city.

FOSTER, STEVENS & CO'S NEW ESTABLISHMENT.

The new establishment which Messrs. Foster, Stevens & Co. are now moving into is perhaps the finest, and, with one or two exceptions in Detroit, the most extensive in the State. The stores have a frontage of 50 feet and a depth of 150 feet. They are connected together by two large arches on each floor. The light is abundant, and the different departments of the new establishment present a very fine appearance. The stores are both four stories, besides a spacious and well lighted basement, which is divided into two parts by the alley, over which the building is arched.

There are two front entrances, Nos. 10 and 12 Monroe street. The first leads to the hardware department on the main floor, where the heavier goods are kept. The second leads to the stove department, the whole floor of this store being used for the exposition of these goods. In the rear of the main floors are located the general offices of the establishment, and also the private office. In connection with these is a very large burglar and fire proof vault. These offices are divided from the salesrooms by a glass partition, thus giving a view of both stores from the offices.

The ascent to the second floor is made by an easy staircase. Here will be found the glass department, the sample room for the wholesale trade, the shelf goods, etc.

On the third floor are the agricultural implements, the tinware department and the work-shops. The fourth floor is to be used for a general warehouse, and the basement for the storage of heavy goods. A steam elevator will make the ascent from floor to floor of this immense establishment, easy and agreeable.

The growth of this house is a matter of astonishment. There are hundreds of pioneers in this city who can remember Mr. W. D. Foster's little tin-shop which was then all that constituted the establishment. It is now one of the leading hardware houses in the Northwestern States. It is not our purpose here to follow the success of this house step by step. The people are familiar with its reputation, and its accomplishments. It will suffice to say that it is now, in all respects, in keeping with, and, perhaps, in advance of the growth of the city of Grand Rapids.

In the next edition of this work, which is to be published next month, containing a more complete history of the county and city, I shall give a detailed history of the Foster estate.

ALDRICH'S BANK.

Although Mr. Aldrich cannot be called one of the pioneers of Grand Rapids, (having came to this city in 1855) still, the enterprise and energy which has marked his career since coming here closely identified him with the rapid growth and improvement of the city.

When Mr. Aldrich first came to Grand Rapids, he engaged in the manufacture of fanning mills, pumps, etc., the sales of the business amounting to over $70,000 yearly.

In 1861 he commenced the banking business, in company with Mr. Ledyard, under the firm name of Ledyard & Aldrich.   In 1862 he sold his interest in the bank to Henry Fralick.   After that the bank of Ledyard & Fralick was changed to the City National, in which Mr. Aldrich became one of the principal stock-holders, also, one of the Directors.

In 1867 Mr. Aldrich was elected Mayor, and was re-elected twice, serving the city three years in all.

In 1871, Mr. Aldrich opened his bank, where he still continues to do business, and is well and favorably known by all classes.

DR. E. WOODRUFF.

This gentleman, who is now a botanic physician in this city, came to this State in May, 1836.   He is a native of Courtland county, N. Y.   After he came to Michigan he remained one year in the village of Barneyville, Calhoun county, (now known as Homer); at that time the village contained one store and one tavern.

A description of the many scenes and incidents of pioneer life in which he took part would fill a large volume.   The Indian feast, the dance, the hunt, games, etc., all of which, when told in his happy style, holds the listener's attention closely bound to his recital.

We have given descriptions of Indian and pioneer life in other parts of this book of which he was an eye witness, and we are indebted to him for much information on many of these subjects.

We find him now, after many years of hardships, quietly enjoying the fruits of his labors.   The profession which he has chosen is alike beneficial to his fellow man, and remunerative to himself.

BIOGRAPHICAL SKETCHES.

JUDGE WITHEY.

Hon. Solomon L. Withey was born in St. Albans, Vermont. He came to Grand Rapids in 1838, and after studying law for some time, he was admitted to the bar. He soon built up a large and profitable practice. In 1848 he was chosen Judge of Probate for Kent county, and held that office for four years. In 1860 he was elected State Senator. Upon the organization of the the Western District of Michigan, in 1863, he was appointed its first United States District Judge, which office he still holds. He is President of the First National Bank of Grand Rapids, and enjoys the respect and confidence of the public.

W. D. FOSTER.

W. D. Foster came to Grand Rapids from Rochester,

N. Y., in the year 1838. He started a small store at the foot of Monroe street in 1845, keeping a general assortment of tin ware, manufactured by himself. His business soon increased, and after several years of great industry he became the leading hardware dealer in western Michigan. He died in the summer of 1873, and his loss was mourned by the whole people. He was a useful, worthy citizen.

HON. P. R. L. PEIRCE.

Hon. P. R. L. Peirce, a native of Genesee, N. Y., came to Grand Rapids in 1840. He studied law in the office of Judge Martin, acting as Deputy County Clerk in 1842–3. In 1853 and 1854 he was City Clerk, and in 1854 he was elected Clerk of Kent county, which office he held during a period of fourteen years. In 1868 he was elected State Senator, in which capacity he proved one of the most influential men from this part of the State. He is now serving the people of Grand Rapids in the high office of Mayor.

REV. JAMES BALLARD.

This gentleman came to Grand Rapids in 1837. He is a native of Charlemont, Massachusetts, and a graduate of William's College of that State. He was pastor of the Congregational church of Grand Rapids for ten years, and the untiring zeal and enterprise displayed by him during that time will always associate his memory with that society. His faithful and untiring efforts in behalf of his flock are clearly proved by the fact that he undertook and performed a journey of over seventeen hundred miles, on foot and alone, through the Eastern States to raise funds to purchase a building for a church.

His noble efforts were rewarded with complete success.

Mr. Ballard has, at different times, held the office of Principal in the Union Schools of Grand Rapids, and at the present time is State agent for the Freedmen's Aid Society, in which office he still continues to labor for the benefit of his fellow men.

A. DIKEMAN.

A. Dikeman came to Grand Rapids in 1837 and commenced the watch and jewelry business, when there were not more than thirteen houses in the place. In 1855 he was joined in partnership by Mr. Bolza, and in 1857 Mr. Bolza left and Mr. Dikeman continued the business tell 1864, when Mr. Parks joined him in a partnership which lasted about four years. In 1866 Mr. Ed. B. Dikeman, his son, purchased a third interest, and in 1867 Mr. A. Dikeman retired. In 1869 Mr. Ed. B. Dikeman purchased the entire interest, which he has carried on since, being now at No. 38 Canal street.

DR. H. G. SAUNDERS.

Dr. Saunders came to Michigan in the fall of 1854, and traveled along the shore of the lake as far north as Pentwater, and located 1,500 acres of land. At that time there were two small mills and boarding houses at Pentwater. The Doctor came to Grand Rapids in 1858 and has practiced here since; also in the government claim and insurance business, in which he has been quite successful. Dr. Saunders has long been interested in real estate and fruit growing, and was the first President of the State Pomological Society, organized in 1870.

HON. LUCIUS LYON.

Among the number of those who contributed not a

little to the "opening up" of the future of this city was the Hon. Lucius Lyon, one of the proprietors, with the late Hon. Charles H. Carroll, of that part of the city called Kent Plat. Believing that salt could be made here, and knowing that this section indicated, geologically, saline springs, he, in 1841, commenced sinking a well on the west bank of the canal, above the big mill, which, after many difficulties and embarrassments, became a supposed success, and the manufacture of salt was, in 1843–4 and 5, prosecuted with considerable spirit, by means of boiling and evaporating. But it failed of being profitable, owing to the difficulties in keeping out fresh water which diluted the brine. We believe Mr. Lyon expended upwards of $20,000 in this experiment, and his profits were nothing. Subsequently, in 1858 to 1864, Messrs. Ball & McKee, J. W. Winsor, W. T. Powers, C. W. Taylor, and the late James Scribner, with others, renewed the effort to make salt, and several wells were sunk, and several thousand barrels made, but East Saginaw had, in the meantime, found the "Seat of Empire," and, from superior and purer brine, soon demonstrated that she was "master of the situation," and our people could not compete with her, and the works in this city gradually went the way of all unprofitable enterprises.

HORTON BROS. & CO.

This is a new firm, which commenced the subscription book business in Grand Rapids in October, 1873. They have been eminently successful in establishing a large business, and have now engaged under their supervision a large number of agents. Their present office is at 69 Bronson street, but we understand they contemplate opening an office "down town" at an early day.   Mr. Fred. L. Horton, the leading partner of the firm, is an active, energetic man, who can scarcely fail of success. Under his supervision over two thousand copies of the "History of Michigan" were sold in Grand Rapids.

CONTENTS.

CHAPTER XX. PAGE.

INDEX TO ADVERTISERS.

THE

FIRST NATIONAL BANK,

GRAND RAPIDS, MICH.

CAPITAL,	- -	$400,000
SURPLUS,	- - -	100,000

OFFICERS:

S. L. WITHEY,	- - -	President.
J. M. BARNETT,	- - -	Vice President.
HARVEY J. HOLLISTER,	- - -	Cashier.

DIRECTORS:

S. L. WITHEY.	W. D. ROBERTS.	WM. A. HOWARD.
JOHN CLANCY.	M. L. SWEET.	T. H. LYON.
J. M. BARNETT.	J. W. CONVERSE.	JAMES BLAIR.

THE
VALLEY CITY PUBLISHING CO.

MANUFACTURERS OF

STANDARD SUBSCRIPTION BOOKS,

OFFICE AND FACTORY,

NO. 21 CANAL ST., - GRAND RAPIDS.

OFFICERS:

MERRILS H. CLARK,	President.
JAMES N. DAVIS,	Vice President.
CORNELIUS A. WALL,	Sec'y and Treas.
CHARLES R. TUTTLE,	Supt.

DIRECTORS.

C. A. WALL.

JAMES N. DAVIS.

M. H. CLARK.

CHARLES R. TUTTLE.

L. B. STANTON.

BOOK AGENTS WANTED.

For all parts of the Northwestern States, for the best selling book in North America. Apply for Territory and particulars to the

VALLEY CITY PUBLISHING CO.,

No. 21 Canal St., GRAND RAPIDS.